IT'S ALWAYS SUNNY
ABOVE THE CLOUDS

Dr. Enfield,

Thank you for your trust and for your
support throughout this writing process.
I could not have done this without you.
Please enjoy the book!,

Nick Tran

IT'S ALWAYS SUNNY ABOVE THE CLOUDS

GETTING THE NEXT GENERATION INTO THE COCKPIT

NICK TRAN

NEW DEGREE PRESS

IT'S ALWAYS SUNNY ABOVE THE CLOUDS

Getting the next generation into the cockpit

ISBN   978-1-63730-362-7 *Paperback*

        978-1-63730-363-4 *Kindle Ebook*

        978-1-63730-364-1 *Ebook*

CONTENTS

———

INTRODUCTION

———

Rule number one: no matter what happens, fly the airplane.

I already knew that. It's the first thing I learned about flying, but it wasn't really helping this time. I drew in a sharp breath, shaking off the anxiousness that every new pilot gets. Slowly, as if my hands would betray my emotion, I took the controls and began taxiing to the runway.

"You need to relax," I told myself. "You're ready for this."

And I was ready. I had done my homework. I knew a lot more than the first rule of flying. I had invested a ton of time and money to get to this point. I felt, or at least I hoped, that I was entering a world in which my possibilities were endless, my potential limitless, and my dreams infinite. I knew it was time. Though I was nervous as hell, I was ready to take my first solo flight.

Many view the world of aviation as they do a mountain—cool to look at, but not something they expect to climb. And, truth be told, there are good reasons behind that. Private pilot numbers have been relatively stagnant for the past decade or so, which is proof that getting your pilot's license is not an easy or quick task. To receive your first aviation license, you must pass tests, complete lessons, and drill concepts, and—to make it harder—none of those things are cheap and all of them are time consuming. A worthwhile commitment, to be sure, but a commitment nonetheless.

On average, a Private Pilot License—that is, the very first license you will acquire—will set you back $10K and will take you seventy hours of pure flying (Pilots Institute 2019). The $10K part cuts out a bunch of prospective pilots right away. In my case, I never could have done it without a scholarship. I would have been overburdened by the simple act of paying for flight school. And that's just the tuition. Next, you have to be able to balance the training and time commitment with the rest of your life. Taking everything into account, you're looking at about a three-month *minimum* commitment. Factor in a lack of diversity and awareness programs, and you get what we have at the moment: an upcoming pilot shortage, and an industry taking decades to evolve.

As you may suspect, having such a high barrier to entry causes problems. Lots of people have "I want to fly a plane" phases, but very few actually do it. Many don't even know where to start. In order for the aviation world to grow, that has to change. The initial costs are overbearing, and the industry suffers as a result. Just ask around in your own circle of friends and family, and you'll probably find someone that considered becoming a pilot long ago but just didn't have the means to do so.

What does that mean for the world above the clouds?

In this modern day and age, 93 percent of our air transport pilots are male and 94 percent of them are white (Bureau of Labor Statistics 2019). The average age of pilots and flight engineers? Forty-four (DataUSA 2018). These and similar statistics indicate a large and compelling problem for the industry, which is old and lacks diversity. It's hardly surprising: with a few exceptions, there is a correlation between whether or not aviation has been in your life previously, how high your income is, and how much free time you have to take on the arduous task of learning to fly. The people who can check off most of these boxes are older white males. What we are experiencing with stagnation in the world of aviation isn't necessarily due to a lack of passion; it's due to a lack of socioeconomic representation.

So where do I fit in, and why am I writing this book?

As the son of immigrant parents from Vietnam, I had the opportunity to grow up with a better life than my parents had. My family, coming to America in 1993, arrived with not much more than their hopes, dreams, and a goal to make sure that their children would live a life of relative luxury. They instilled in me determination, discipline, and opportunity, and I took that mindset with me to the skies. Having flown for the last five years as a pilot, I want to make sure that I make an impact on the aviation community. This is my story: of how I got into flying and how I want to help the next generation of pilots step forward.

As a young pilot of color, I've only seen a couple of others like me. As someone coming from a lower-class background with no connections to the world of flight, the golden gates to flight were seemingly locked. But I managed to succeed, and I want to help others like me achieve their goals. At the same time, I hope this helps to grow the flying community. With any luck, I can draw some attention to the disparity issue as well as present my own path as a model for others. I took the leap into the skies—why not others?

The question isn't whether or not aviation suffers because of the lack of diversity. I would argue that it does. It's also not whether it is my duty to introduce the joys of flight to more people. I think it is, and I'm ready to do that. The real question is *how* to expand the support base that will allow more people to pursue their dreams of flight.

We already know *why* diversity is important. There are numerous studies pointing at the exact same conclusion: diversity allows the world to incorporate new ideas, grow, and advance as a result.

We also know how important it is to get more pilots. As we enter a post–COVID-19 world, a massive shortage of pilots is a key threat against the world of American aviation. Hundreds of flights were canceled this past month by some of the largest airlines in the United States, all due to a lack of pilots.

With an aging pilot workforce facing early retirement, high entry costs, and exponentially growing demand, securing new pilots has become an increasingly worrying challenge. In a 2019 Oliver Wyman poll of air carriers around the world, 62 percent said that a looming shortage of pilots was a primary risk to growth. When the pandemic hit, many carriers opted for early retirement of their pilots—which simply exacerbated the problem. Post–COVID-19, the pilot workforce in many countries is now permanently reduced. In the United States alone, that shortage is projected to be over 12,000 pilots by 2023, with another massive surge of mandatory retirements to come by the end of the decade (OliverWyman 2021).

So we know the problem: aviation is aging and becoming more homogeneous. What about a solution?

It's up to the next generation of pilots to make a grand transformation. How can you get your license (and not drain your bank account completely)? What are some ways that others have broken through the glass ceilings of flight? Why should you care about any of this? It can be comforting to just stick to the status quo as we look at these unprecedented times, but it's now more than ever that we will need to rise up and make a change to ensure the viability of flight.

A world without flight affects all of us, and the aviation community must work together to make sure that our future is set up to continue. We need to show young, diverse pilots that anyone is capable of flight, and that those childhood dreams are closer than ever. We need to explore new ways to lower the barriers to entry so that we can create more pilots, not turn more away. Perhaps the biggest thing of all is that we need to increase awareness: it's hard to be what you can't see. By promoting diverse pilot role models, we can take on the aviation diversity gap and fill it with the ambition of eager, young pilots.

That's why I am writing this book. I want to reach out to those who have always wanted to fly and just never found the way to do so. The pilots of the future will be the ones ensuring the industry succeeds and evolves. This book is for them— those who want to fly, those who want to have an impact on our future, and those who want to make sure that aviation continues to be enjoyable and successful for years to come.

As pilots, we learn to adapt or fail when we fly. Our industry must do the same and adapt along with us. Pilots-to-be, my goal in writing this this book is to set you up with multiple approaches into the world of flight. Ultimately, it's up to you to make it happen. I hope you find some inspiration in these pages, and I hope to see all of you in the sun above the clouds. Good luck, and blue skies!

CHAPTER 1

MY INSPIRATION STORY (HOW I GOT ABOVE THE CLOUDS)

___

We have a saying about flying in the aviation industry: a mile of open road can take you one mile, but a mile of open runway can take you anywhere in the world. This idea—the immense promise the world offered—launched my love of flight.

It wasn't until my first solo flight that I was able to truly comprehend the magnificence of the beautiful sky above us. My little Cessna 150 had taken into the air, as if an invisible giant had plucked it from the ground. This was a combination of centuries of physics, chemistry, and mathematics coming together in one object now completely under my control. Even in my small airplane, the huge expanse that flowed beneath me seemed conquerable. It was all part of my new kingdom as I looked down from above.

As I sat there, surrounded by an aluminum exoskeleton, there came a magnificent feeling, one that had never surfaced before. Alongside all of the wonder and the delight, the sentiment of opportunity shone through, and on I flew, just me and a metal extension of my body.

Flying will always hold a special place in my heart. Not only does it make up about 93 percent of my personality, it also opened my eyes to pure independence. Flying represents my thoughts about the universal pursuit of advancement, my desire to be immersed in a world where my possibilities have no end and my dreams contain immeasurable potential for myself and humanity. This is what defines my character. Flying fulfills this dream for me, bringing with it an insatiable need to expand upon the world and my opportunities. Up there, my ambitions soar; my aspirations take off. Much like the boundless sky, my mind has no limitations.

MY FIRST TIME ABOVE THE CLOUDS

I remember the very first flight that I took as a student. At sixteen years old, I was eager to pursue my childhood dream of flight. With the help of my mom, I called up a local flight school and scheduled a discovery flight (more on these later). For the price of $100, I was able to fly in the left seat of a small Cessna 152 for an entire hour. It was an absolute blast, and it confirmed my interest in aviation even though I was just a sophomore in high school.

The problem, however, came when I inquired about the total cost. Conservative estimates listed it at a cool $10K, and that was with close to minimal training. Coming from an immigrant family whose income was barely above the poverty line, there was absolutely no way I would be able to afford that. I basically had two options—go into debt with a loan before I even entered college, or bankrupt my family—both of which would have absolutely demolished my future.

For most prospective students, the dream ends there. It's a simple equation, with one constant: a lack of opportunity. The main difference for me was that I was a self-proclaimed aviation geek. I knew what I wanted to do and had known it for years. No matter the cost, I would get my pilot's license; if not now, then later. Luckily, later came about a month into my junior year of high school.

I've always been extremely fortunate to have become a pilot. This dream of mine was possible due to a couple of important factors. The first lucky charm I had up my sleeve was my high school: I went to Raisbeck Aviation High School (RAHS), an aerospace/aeronautical STEM-focused school in the Seattle area. A couple of my teachers were pilots, and one was a Certificated Flight Instructor (CFI). I talked to him one day after school and found out that he didn't charge RAHS students for instruction. I would only have to pay for use of the plane. Immediately, my costs were reduced by almost $4K. The flight club plane I would be using was also significantly less expensive than the airplanes at a traditional flight school. This saved me another one or two thousand. Overall, it meant that I could afford to pursue my dream.

Or so I thought.

MONEY, TIME, OR FREE INSTRUCTION

Flying with my first CFI allowed me to afford my passion, but actually being able to pursue it was another thing. I started during winter in Seattle, meaning that it was often too cloudy, too windy, or maybe just too cold to fly. It didn't help that I had little time to dedicate toward training. On top of my homework and other clubs, flying just didn't look like it was going to work out. The cost savings were there, but the time wasn't. In addition to my lack of availability, my CFI also had to train for his own Flight Review so he could continue to instruct. The timing just wasn't working, and after an agonizing four months, I thought I was going to have to quit flying.

There I was, walking into my CFI's classroom right at the end of the school year. As I entered, there was someone there that I had never met before. Before I could say the words, "I don't think our schedules are working out," my CFI spoke up. This stranger in the room, Joseph Merlino, was an alumnus of my high school. Better yet, he had recently received his license to teach and was looking for new aviation students to start in the upcoming summer.

This was perfect. Not only was the weather fantastic in the summer but so were our schedules. We flew together every day, and flying slowly began to feel like second nature. Go to work, go to the airport, hop in a plane, and fly. Rinse and repeat. I learned a massive amount, and the everyday use of my new skills reinforced them in my mind. My confidence in flight shot up. We accelerated through my training, and were about a month out from scheduling my checkride when time caught up to us once again. We made it through about 80 percent of my training before Joseph had to head back to school.

So in the fall of senior year, I was stuck without an instructor. I searched and searched for a flight school that had any sort of availability, but it wasn't until two months later that I could finally get off a waitlist and into a program. Two months without flying meant my skills had gone down the drain, and I practically had to start over. Not great news.

I started flying again with Dart, an ex–flight attendant pursuing his flying dreams, and he worked hard to get me caught up. Before too long, though, Dart had received an offer with a private jet company and made the leap to pursue his passion. I would fly with him again soon enough, but for the time being, I once again needed an instructor.

The flight school assigned me another CFI a month later, but unfortunately, he was not checked out in the Cessna 152 (the most affordable plane available), so I couldn't fly with him. After a month of just doing ground lessons (my skills were totally gone at this point), I was burning through what little funding I had left. I was starting to question whether I would ever get my license.

Enter Rachel, my fifth and final CFI. By the time we met, it had been about five months from when I last flew. So, I had the time, and I had the instructor. This time, though, I was without the benefit of cheap flight time and free instruction. In other words, after five months of being grounded, I no longer had the money.

Fortunately for me, there was hope. My good grades and determination won me an interview for a $10,000 scholarship to finish my license; I pulled through and secured the scholarship. With money, weather, and time out of the way, I was able to get it all done and earned my license on September 21, 2019.

My path to success was a long and winding one, and it is one that would make most people wash out of any program. But that isn't the takeaway I want you to have. The point that I want to emphasize is this: I didn't have a plan before it all started. I was trying to figure things out as I went. This meant that when I got stuck without an instructor, everything that I had learned was basically thrown away. It was essentially a restart. Hell, even with a plan, half of my story was a result of an unexpected obstacle. That is why I felt compelled to write this book and offer others a plan that I never had. I don't want anyone to make my mistakes. I don't want anyone to waste both time and a few thousand dollars.

CHAPTER 2

THE CURRENT STATE OF AVIATION

———

We've been flying airplanes for over a century now. We've been eyeing the skies for millennia before that. So how far have we come? The world above the clouds is sunny, to be sure—but not everyone is able to get there. Aviation has never been more accessible, and yet, the industry is stagnant, and our numbers are reflective of a fly in a bowl of milk.

POST–COVID-19

You're hired.

That was the phrase most aspiring pilots heard when they applied for a job. Before COVID-19 hit, and before pilot jobs began to disappear from thin air, the world was facing a *massive* pilot shortage. Airlines and the Air Force alike were in a huge panic. To meet growing demand, the United States would need to "train a staggering 87 new pilots every day—for the next 20 years" (Emsi 2018). Companies were beginning to offer huge signing bonuses—up to and above $42,100—just to get more qualified pilots into their planes to keep up with the staggering demand for air travel. Pre-pandemic forecasts from Boeing showed that the world would need an estimated 637,000 new pilots by the year of 2036 (CNN 2017).

Then came the pandemic. COVID-19 completely reversed that trend, with companies barely being able to keep pilots on payroll. Pilot jobs disappeared overnight, leaving many in the industry floundering. But fast forward to now: more and more vaccines have been distributed, and airlines are estimating that the demand for pilots is about to make a massive comeback. That's happening just when many pilots were pushed into early retirement due to the pandemic. The shortage will only be felt harder and stronger. Recent data from CAE Inc. estimates that despite the industry slump, the world will continue to need 264,000 pilots over this coming decade (CAE 2020). In short: the aviation industry desperately needs more people in the flight deck, period.

THE FINANCIAL PROBLEM
Statistically, the majority of people that start their flight training never finish it. When you are a student pilot, it's easy to see why. For many reasons, the field of aviation can be seemingly impenetrable. Firstly, it takes a lot of time and effort to obtain your license. Not only do you have to cram seemingly random regulations into your brain, but you also need to know when those laws are applied and why they exist. Along with these rules comes a lot of interpretation, establishment of personal minimums, memorization of proper

flying procedures, recognition of unofficial flying procedures, decision making under pressure—the list goes on. And in case you think you can get away with simply flying the plane well, just know that you are tested on three things at the end of your training: your flying ability is only one of them. Your ability to regurgitate and explain these flight laws both on a proctored written exam and in a multi-hour oral exam are the other two.

So let's say that, as a student pilot, you grind your way through hours of ground school and pick up quickly on the actual flying. The problem now is money. Pilots always joke about it, but flying takes a lot of money. Flight training can often seem like an endless black hole specifically targeting your wallet. In fact, according to a 2010 study by the Aircraft Owners and Pilots Association (AOPA), in a survey of one thousand pilots, costs and financing were listed as the largest negative factor of receiving training. This was higher up than bad instructors, a lack of aircraft availability, and even the difficulty of receiving a license in general.

To further prove my point, if you were to go online and find any old "How to Get Your License" article, almost all of the comments will talk about the difficulties of affording flight time. A 2014 article by Sporty's Student Pilot News' Charlie Masters breaks down the four biggest reasons why many pilots give up on their goals, starting with—you guessed it—money.

Charlie began taking lessons back when he was in college. He would work some, fly until he was broke, and then go back and earn more money. "During each layoff, whether for a few weeks or a few months, I lost my skills which required more time and more money being spent than if I would have been able to complete my training in a single session," he writes. "Unfortunately, flying is not an activity for the thin of wallet."

The average cost of training ranges anywhere from $7,000 to $15,000, and that is just so you can fly your friends around on a nice sunny day. Most people don't have that kind of money sitting in their pocket, so they often do a pay-as-you-go program. They pay for each flight lesson immediately after they finish it. So when you're in the middle of your training and hit a plateau, you may as well be burning money—and at approximately $200+ an hour to fly with an instructor, most of us begin to question whether our end goal is achievable. It is the harsh reality of this field. As a result of price discrimination, most pilots-to-be are stuck with nothing more than a dream.

THE AWARENESS PROBLEM

Okay, Google, how do I become a pilot? From myths about plane crash statistics to the various complexities of flight, few people know much about the flourishing aviation community. It's a major reason why aviation is such a small field: we aren't well advertised outside of our small networks.

Think about what it is like to get your driver's license. It is practically an expectation in the United States, with over 230 million citizens obtaining one—that is 70 percent of our population (Statistica 2020). Thanks to the popularity of the driver's license, people know how to go about getting one, and thanks to the capacity for long distance travel and the economics of car ownership, society sees the viability and reason behind getting a driver's license.

Getting your pilot's license, however, is an entirely different animal. While a little over 50 percent of Americans say they have flown at least once in the past year, most people don't know the first thing about obtaining your pilot's license (Air-SpaceMag 2016). It's not advertised in everyday life, and even when you do fly, the flight attendants and pilots don't really explain everything going on.

It's not just an issue for pilots—the industry projects that "there will be more than two million more employees needed in the aviation and aerospace industries over the next twenty years" (FAA 2021). In order to keep up with record-breaking numbers for air travel (once we recover from the pandemic, of course), airlines will continue to need pilots, technicians, and engineers at a record-breaking pace—and we have seen airlines go bankrupt over a lack of employees before. For the next generation going into the aviation industry, we can expect salaries and benefits to go way up as a direct result of the soon-to-come shortage of aviation personnel.

The biggest issue is making sure that the pilots of the future understand that. A lack of awareness is a huge reason why many people are not motivated to seriously consider getting up in the air themselves. In other words, unless you know about your opportunities, there isn't really a chance for you to achieve what you want. It's a major reason why more people don't end up pursuing their dreams. They don't know how to go about accomplishing them. After all, why pursue something if you don't know how it works?

THE DIVERSITY PROBLEM

Today, the aviation industry is a mosh pit of pilots from different backgrounds—just kidding. From the engineering side to the flying, there is one predominant group—older, rich, white males. This isn't inherently a bad thing, but 93 percent of pilots are males, 94 percent of pilots are white, and more than 30 percent of pilots in the current industry fall within the age range of fifty to sixty-four years old, and such statistics leave very little room for progress and diversification (BLS 2019, PilotInstitute 2020).

First off, let's look at the issue of diversity, or rather, the lack of it. Diversity comes in all shapes and sizes—race, sex, culture, and age—and all of those traits come together to change the world. Studies routinely show that diversity is a beneficial factor in industry and community. Overall, it enhances creativity and encourages us as humans to search for new information and perspectives, leading to evolution, better decision making, and unique problem solving. According to a 2013 Organization for Economic Cooperation and Development (OECD) study of 24,000 research and development institutes, more diverse research teams submitted more patent applications and brought increased revenue and product innovation to their organizations (NBAA 2018).

It's not hard to see how this line of thinking directly applies to the world of aviation. As pilots, we constantly adapt to changing conditions. Not only are we trained to correct problems, we're expected to solve them under stress. Aviation safety is dependent not only on unity in the flight deck but on unity throughout the industry. Having more pilots from different backgrounds working together on issues that face aviation can only help. In fact, a study by Egon Zehnder, a global management consulting firm, showed that "the top-performing airlines have a significantly higher diversity of leadership across all of our eight diversity criteria." Says Christoph Wahl, the global segment leader of Air Transport & Aviation, "[These] low-cost airlines notably have a higher proportion of women in senior roles and are more ready to bring in outsiders with cross-industry experience.... [this] diversity in its broadest sense is a powerful weapon against group-think and can drive commercial success in changing markets" (FlightGlobal 2016). Given the data and statistics, there is absolutely no reason why we shouldn't promote aviation to those that have been traditionally left out of the picture.

With these diversification efforts come something that the entirety of the industry needs right now: pilots. If we continue on our current path, we effectively limit the world's access to new aviation talent, hindering our overall ability to meet aviation demand. We need to get more people in the air, and that begins with opening the doors to groups that have been previously locked out of the room.

To understand the problem, we need to understand our history. America has always had a problem with discrimination, and that unfortunately includes its military. This seems like a random connection until you realize that the military supplied the majority of our nation's pilots all the way up through the Vietnam War. However, it wasn't until WWII that the military began to train Black pilots, and it was decades later, in 1974, when women were finally able to enter the military cockpit. Even then, it definitely wasn't a career path that was encouraged for these diverse groups. That meant aviation was pretty homogeneous, and in plain words, it was largely known as a job for white males.

Fast forward a couple of years. Those white, male pilots trained by the military began to encourage their sons to get into the cockpit. They had an understandable desire to share their passions with their family. Back then, aviation programs specifically designed to get people of color flying didn't really exist. It was America in the '70s, so racism most definitely played a role in that. As a result, the aviation industry welcomed more and more white pilots, and very few additional pilots of color or female pilots. Unfortunately, this is a cycle that continues today.

These days, we're an advanced society and have the knowledge of one. We know that pilots of color and pilots of any gender, sex, or religion are able to fly just as well as anyone. So why don't we see more diversity in our respective field? You can't be what you can't see, the saying goes. Capturing the eyes of young potential pilots, particularly ones from different backgrounds, goes a long way when encouraging diversity in our cockpits. The world already sees and knows that white men are able to be pilots, but what the world doesn't yet see nearly as much are pilots of color, LGBTQ+ pilots, and female pilots doing the very same thing. Imagining yourself flying is a lot harder when you can't even imagine someone that *looks* like you flying.

Without more diversity in the field, there is less motivation for pilots of color and female pilots, effectively discouraging them from experiencing the joys of flight. Pilot Patrick sums up the situation quite well: "During one of my first lessons with the DA20 [a type of plane], my flight instructor looked at me and said, 'Patrick, you have to know: women and Black people have no place in the cockpit.'" This lack of acceptance and diversity is seen throughout the world of aviation, often implicitly, Patrick continues. At his first job with a small charter company, only white men sat in the cockpit. His second job, at a company of about double the size, employed two women. Even when he began work at a large German airline, he found that women, people of color, and members of the LGBTQ+ community were significantly underrepresented. It was only after six years of flying that he finally flew with a female captain, and he has yet to fly with a Black colleague (Pilot Patrick 2020).

Luckily, where aviation falls short, the world makes up for it (sometimes). Recent initiatives to get female pilots and pilots of color are more common than ever, with major airlines and companies prioritizing diversity and inclusion through financial efforts. Among those initiatives is United Airlines' Aviate program, which aims to enroll 5,000 students by 2030, half of which are women and pilots of color. Backed by scholarship commitments totaling $2.4 million from United Airlines and JPMorgan Chase, the academy will create opportunities for thousands of students to pursue a career as a commercial airline pilot (United Airlines Press Release 2021).

Additionally, as United pilot Carole Hopson notes, the effort will go a long way in reducing the massive opportunity gap in aviation, as well as reducing the sexist remarks that are endured by many female pilots.

"Even when I'm in my full pilot's uniform, passengers will ask me for a cup of coffee and confuse me for a flight attendant, as if that is the only job a woman can have on a plane," she says. Many people, if they don't say anything, often gawk. Hopson does note, however, that a few are amazed, such as the young mother who pulled Hopson aside to ask how her daughter could follow in Hopson's footsteps. According to Hopson, the initiative by United Aviate and its partners will "hopefully allow other Black women to experience the thrill of flight, and inspire more children of color to consider careers in aviation" (People 2021).

So how do we address this?

One of the best things about the aviation community today is the familial aspect—aviators are some of the most well-connected people I have ever met (as we should be, since each one of us is able to bond over the fact that we climbed a metaphorical mountain). It's important, then, for us to use this community to encourage others to fly. We can do this by hosting flight events and promoting the idea that aviation is a possibility for all aspiring pilots. That last part is particularly important, and the best way to do this is by placing diverse pilots in positions to be role models. This way, pilots get the most out of their efforts. We don't need to talk about this issue so much as put the picture out there, making it known that anyone can fly.

CHAPTER 3

DIGITAL COMMUNITIES

———

One of the most notable things about the aviation industry is the strength of its community. Once you're officially in, you want to bond with others who have made it through the program, as aviation is one of the most interconnected communities on Earth.

BRICE VAN BAREN AND
THE "FLIGHTS ABOVE" COMMUNITY

It may not surprise you to hear that there's quite a large aviation community on social media. One of the largest organizations is the Flights Above group. I wanted to explore this area of flying because I knew from personal experience that this group and others like it are fantastic resources for potential pilots. Luckily, I was able to snag an interview with Brice Van Baren, founder of Flights Above and a media creator at his company, Positive Rate Media.

Brice had gotten his start with aviation back in 1986, with a new game that was all the rage back then: Microsoft Flight Simulator. His dad, an aviation enthusiast, taught his sons how to fly the sim "religiously—to him, it wasn't just a game!" Evidently, it worked. Brice began to really enjoy his time in the simulator, and the rest is history. He worked hard to get his pilot's license in real life after he had caught the flying bug from his old home computer.

After that, he felt only one thing was missing.

"I had been flying for three years at the time, Nick, and I was running into this problem—I was having a hard time making any lasting connections in aviation."

This was a really interesting point, because even in the first minutes of our interview, Brice exuded friendliness and confidence. He seemed to me like the exact type of person that you would want to become friends with, and it was surprising that he didn't find any strong relationships as he flew—and as it turns out, he was surprised by it as well. And so, Brice decided to do something about it.

As Brice recalled, in February of 2012, Facebook had recently released this new feature: Facebook groups.

"I was thinking to myself, well, this could be fun, so let me go ahead and create one."

As he played around with the app, he came up with a fun and easy-to-remember nickname: Flights Above the Pacific Northwest—or FATPNW, as it's lovingly called today. He invited his old instructors and a couple of other pilots he knew, and they proceeded to invite their students and friends. That first night, a total of twelve people were on FATPNW, sharing their aviation stories and posting envy-inducing pictures of their sleek aircrafts.

What Brice didn't expect, though, was how much the group would explode.

"That first night, we were twelve, and the next day, we were at thirty-five. Which is like, yeah, that's normal—but then a week later, we were at two hundred."

To give you an idea of how large the group is now, FATPNW recently celebrated its twenty thousandth member—and that's just in the Pacific Northwest region. As the group expanded, Brice created more for the different areas that existed: Flights Above now has a North Central States region, a Pacific Southwest region, and in just about every other area in the United States, they've got a region and a group for it.

Brice is quick to point out, however, that the size of the group wasn't what was important. It was all about the growth.

"To me, that indicated a niche market. Pilots wanted to mingle with each other; they wanted to connect and share their stories."

To that end, Brice made it Flights Above's goal to give the people what they wanted. Each season, the FATPNW community would have a major event, whether that be a fly-in, an airshow, or a tower visit. And every season, people flocked to these events. They did so to meet old friends, to connect with new friends, and to celebrate aviation. Friendships were made instantly, and they shared the unbreakable bond of the spirit of aviation.

As we proceeded through the interview, I was able to gather Brice's own thoughts on the state of aviation as it currently exists—a rather interesting perspective because of the position he has with the Flights Above community. Just like his Facebook group, Brice is excited about aviation's potential to grow. Along with an overall explosion of pilots from 2009 to 2020, there is also a huge shift in diversity and inclusion. Those, alongside the statistics Brice had from managing the Flights Above group, were fantastic indicators of interest. "I mean, just look at the traffic we have in the Seattle area. Just take a look at the traffic pattern around Renton—that should tell you how big general aviation has become."

While there has been overall growth in the past decade, however, something that concerns Brice is the ever-increasing cost of flight. The way he dealt with this issue is quite an innovative idea.

"Within Flights Above, we have the option for a premium membership. This premium membership unlocks huge discounts and services at FBOs (flight-based operations) across the nation."

The notion is simple. As a pilot, you would pay an annual premium of ninety-nine dollars. In return, you would receive up to 15 percent discounts on aviation-related purchases at partnering companies (saving you hundreds and possibly thousands of dollars). Seeing as parts in aviation are always more expensive than you would think, these discounts could save aircraft owners thousands—and at the same time, promote business for these aviation companies. It's a fantastic way to keep costs down, and keep the aviation economy flowing.

Diversity has also been much better in these Facebook groups, according to Brice.

"What we're seeing is an increase in women in our groups, and an increase in pilots of different nationalities and religions joining our flying community."

While Brice acknowledges that there is a long way to go, the groups help minority pilots find and connect with one another and gain some representation in an industry where they are drastically underrepresented.

I know from experience that the online aviation community can truly help new pilots learn. I know because I wasn't afraid to ask questions to some of these more experienced aviators. I was able to quickly gain local knowledge about a specific airport, which made my flight safer. I was also able to give my own two cents on aviation to pilots that were still in the process of receiving their license. Many others in the group did the same, asking and answering questions for others. In all, this was a very helpful group that encouraged giving back to the community.

Flights Above was also a great group in terms of fitting in. It was a group where I found other Asian—and not only Asian, but Vietnamese—pilots. Throughout all of my training, this had never happened before. It was a group where I could proudly share my achievements (like how my Instrument

Checkride Success post received 300+ likes, and the comments were full of well wishes and overall support). Overall, the group demonstrated just how interactive the aviation community is and how exciting it is to be a part of such a tight-knit family.

Brice had his own story about that as well.

"One of our smaller fly-in events brought us into the middle of nowhere, to an airfield where everyone could hunker down and set up some tents. We're there for a couple days, you know, all having fun and talking to one another, and all of a sudden, a freak sandstorm came up out of nowhere."

Needless to say, the airplanes (and the tents) didn't do so well.

"One of the poles ripped off and basically tore an entire windscreen off of one of our planes. Luckily, not much else was damaged, but there was just no way this guy was gonna be able to get home!"

And here, folks, is where the beauty of the aviation community comes in. A small group of pilots flew back to civilization (where they had cell service) and proceeded to send out an alert to the Flights Above community.

"You know, they flew out, typed up the message on the way, and sent it out as soon as they landed. I'm telling you now—within the hour, we had a rescue crew on their way."

The community rallied together. They sent out a local pilot and a trusty mechanic, along with tools and a new windscreen. This was all the way to an airport in the middle of nowhere. Within the day, everyone that attended the event was able to make it back home safe and sound—with tighter bonds to one another than ever before. That was when Brice truly knew he had created something great. The small family that started as a twelve-person group had grown into a nationwide community. And together as a community, it had the opportunity to do great (and fun) things.

But the reason I wanted to tell this story wasn't just to show you that the world of flight is a tight-knit place. I wanted to emphasize the ability that aviators have to change the world around them. The windscreen story truly goes to show the faith that pilots place in one another, and that principle in itself highlights exactly why the aviation industry has room to grow. Technology brings us together and gives us the opportunity to expand and advocate for ourselves. It also provides us with the ability to reach new, diverse youth and get them up and into the cockpit. It allows us to share our stories, like Brice shared his with me, and then work together to make flying more equitable.

Simply put, flying doesn't have to be as exclusive as it currently is. In fact, this book is full of stories about people who have broken that cloud layer and the stories that they were able to make along the way. All their tales serve this primary idea that it is time for the next generation of pilots to step up and learn their roles. Effectively, these new pilots are able to inject the industry with a figurative breath of fresh air by introducing their technologically incorporated ideas and progressive lifestyles to the industry. With them comes the potential for faster planes, safer planes, and overall better planes. There is no reason why we should allow pilots to become a thing of the past, and the best way to ensure this is by promoting the pilots of the future.

CHAPTER 4

GETTING STARTED

———

Alright—we've covered some of the issues of aviation now, but how do we fix them? Let's start with an overview of aviation advocacy—primarily, local aviation clubs that help get more young and diverse pilots up into the skies. Making sure that younger pilots are aware of the aviation world is how we get pilots interested in the first place. To demonstrate this, I want to introduce the Experimental Aircraft Association (EAA) and one of its local chapter directors in Traverse City, Michigan.

EXPERIMENTAL AIRCRAFT

Experimental aircraft. When we first think of those words, cool and exotic aircraft come to mind—aircraft that break the sound barrier, that look weird and strange as NASA attempts to test some new technology. As such, many of us are surprised to think about just how common experimental aircraft are, and just how popular they have come to be. Out of 167,000 general aviation aircraft, 34,200 of them are experimental, or about 1 in every 5 planes (FAA 2020).

So why are there so many of these "experimental" planes flying around? Are they safe? Who flies them?

Experimental aircraft are a bit of a misnomer. Under FAA regulations, if an individual builds at least 51 percent of an aircraft, the aircraft is able to be registered in the "amateur-built" category. This category happens to be licensed by the FAA as "experimental," meaning they can only be used for recreational purposes. This experimental designation has been in existence for more than five decades, and other than a Private Pilot License, there is nothing else that you would need to fly one of these planes.

That may sound dangerous, but while there are a couple of "truly experimental aircraft that are originally designed, the overwhelming majority are built using standardized, tried-and-true kits or plans that have been successfully constructed thousands of times" (EAA 2021)

When these aircraft were first being built back in the '50s, the FAA didn't have an official category for the aircraft. They weren't "factory-built," like their Cessna and Piper peers, and they also didn't qualify as military planes or airliners. The FAA then came up with a clever solution, designating the aircraft as "experimental," and simply creating a new subcategory called "amateur-built." Fun fact—most aircraft that are not popular enough to get their own category are put underneath this experimental category. This includes about ten other subcategories, such as market survey demonstrators, air racing, and historical aircraft flown to air shows and exhibitions.

At any rate, the category is primarily dominated by the world of general aviation, with many aviators choosing this path to save both money and time.

A huge part of why flying is so expensive is because it is an absolutely unforgiving hobby—make one mistake and it could end your life. As a result, the FAA requires all production aircraft to be thoroughly tested: everything must undergo intensive certification processes that ensure the airplane will continue to fly even when you push it to the limits. Everything must be tested—from the flaps to the belts that drive the engine—under all possible conditions (heat, ice, stress, you name it). While this makes sense, it becomes incredibly expensive to then bring new products to market (AINOnline 2006). Not only are the certification organizations' fees insanely high, but each test requires more than just one prototype. And if anything fails, it must go back to the drawing board. As a result, what could have been a five-cent bolt (singular, mind you) may very well cost upwards of ten dollars.

That is where these experimental aircraft excel—because they do not require all the testing, designing, and scrutiny of a new production aircraft. That doesn't mean that experimental aircraft don't require inspections, though. All aircraft must be inspected by an FAA or designated inspector before an airworthiness certificate can be issued, and the builder must provide logs, supporting documents, and photographs of the build process. Then, they must fly between twenty-five to forty hours of test flights in non-populated areas to ensure all components work properly. Additionally, once registered, experimental aircraft must undergo all the normal inspections that a production aircraft requires for general operations. As a result, studies by the National Transportation Safety Board (NTSB) and the FAA show that accident rates for experimental aircraft are less than one percentage point higher than the general aviation fleet, even as the number of registered aircraft have doubled and total hours flown have skyrocketed by 123 percent (EAA 2021).

In many cases, experimental aircraft become more efficient to fly because of how much liberty the pilot has with their airplane. Modifications can include state-of-the-art instrumentation and fancy glass cockpits—even smaller parts such as extra radios and audio jacks. If anything, the experimental category allows you to be safer. There are nice touch screen panels that display all necessary information, digitized instruments that warn you when something may be going wrong, and GPS displays that alert you to other aircraft traffic. These all help increase situational awareness, and only experimental aircraft owners are able to get them installed without the multi-thousand-dollar price tags.

Then, to drive it all home, there's overall cost. Instead of $80,000 for an old aircraft, there are many experimental aircraft kits that go for less than $20,000! Most experimental aircraft also utilize composite materials that make them lighter, faster, and more fuel efficient than similar production aircraft, according to the EAA. Experimental aircraft offer an inexpensive way to enter aviation and a great way to truly understand the mechanics of flight.

THE EXPERIMENTAL AIRCRAFT ASSOCIATION (EAA)

The Experimental Aircraft Association has been around for over half a century now, and it is a growing and diverse aviation organization that deals with just about everything that flies. One of the largest existing flight communities, the EAA prides itself on the "spirit of aviation." It offers pilots the opportunity to take to the skies in any way they want through workshops, rallies, and overall community support. They have extensive guides on building your own aircraft and getting into the aviation industry, and most famously, they host the world's busiest air event: Oshkosh AirVenture.

Naturally, such a major player in the business of aviation advocacy has a special place in this book. To solidify that, I was given the fantastic opportunity to speak with Sarah Pagano—director of an EAA chapter in Traverse City, Michigan—about her flight path and how the Young Eagles program could help others find their passions as aviators.

Sarah originally worked on an airfield, setting up hot-air balloons during the hot Michigan summers. As a child, she loved NASA and loved the idea of space. When they noticed this determination, Sarah's parents were able to sign her up for a special aviation day camp at EAA chapter 1093—a flourishing Young Eagle's program that would get Sarah from watching planes to flying them. Sarah absolutely loved the camp. It propelled her to pursue a degree in aviation management and gave her what she calls her dream job: she's now the camp director of the very camp that she signed up for as a child.

For Sarah, the best part of the EAA is being able to fulfill children's dreams of flying. Promoting women in the industry, presenting opportunities for interested children with autism and Cerebral Palsy into the cockpit, and hosting aviation education days for specialized youth groups in general are great ways to promote diversity and inclusion in our world above the clouds. Sarah's chapter does all that and more, including offering scholarships to young people interested in the world of flight. That program is essential. She states, "Cost is always a barrier to flight—the EAA helps tear that barrier down."

What truly stands out for Sarah is the representation that these EAA programs provide. "There is saying to people, 'You can do anything you believe in,' and then there is showing them that reality. With EAA, I'm able to show them their dreams are achievable." As we talked, Sarah beamed from her camp's accomplishment. She recalled a specific time a grateful father came up to her and let her know just how inspiring she was to his young daughters. They were able to see women in a position of power, seeing women behind the controls of a plane for the first time in their lives. Sarah remembered just how proud she felt. She was a role model. She had set a powerful example for those young women.

We spoke on the topic of her education days as well. A particular camp for at-risk students especially stood out to her. After these students went through a quick presentation on aviation and all the ways it could impact their lives, they were given the opportunity to climb into the cockpit and apply their knowledge, earning themselves a certificate of completion. She began to tear up as she told the story of how excited the students were and brought up another memory she would never forget. As the last aircraft landed and shut down, she went to debrief the final student, who was absolutely beaming. He had a huge grin on his face as he proudly held his freshly printed certificate out and quipped, "Now my mom finally has something good from me to put up on the fridge." It's moments like those, she laughed, that inspire her to continue.

THE YOUNG EAGLES FLIGHT PROGRAM
AND OTHER ADVOCACY GROUPS

Perhaps the best part of the EAA for prospective pilots is their Young Eagles flight program. By offering prospective and young students a free opportunity to get behind the wheel (yoke? stick?) of an aircraft, the program truly encourages more people to get involved in the world of flight. For over twenty-five years, Young Eagles (youth from eight to seventeen years old) have been able to take a free introductory flight made possible by local community pilots. These dedicated volunteers are essential to the program, introducing the next generation of passionate and curious aviators to a brand-new way of viewing the world. Students would come out from all over the state to get a chance to fly—and for many of them, once they got into the air, they never wanted to come back down.

Young Eagles may be the EAA's flagship program for youth, but they don't stop there. EAA aviation days are happening all over the country, pushing aviation advocacy to new heights. Oshkosh AirVenture attracts pilots from all over the country, all flying into the small town of Oshkosh, Wisconsin for a weeklong flying convention. The small regional airport there becomes the world's busiest airfield for those couple of days, with approximately 134 takeoffs and landings in the span of an hour for over seven days straight. According to the EAA, more than 10,000 aircraft fly in, over 600,000 visitors attend, and the event is only getting bigger. If you have the option, take an online look at a recorded flight into Oshkosh—controllers switch off rapidly, and the communications to aircraft don't stop. Pilots aren't even given the option to respond, as there simply is not enough time for them to talk.

Of course, all of this commotion is a perfect place to introduce people to the world of flight. What better way to captivate a young audience than with the startling roar of fighter jets or unique performance planes doing tricks and spins in the blue sky? Oshkosh also provides the perfect stage for WomenVenture, a series of events at Oshkosh that is essential to forming the sense of community that is so strong with pilots. This event highlights the feats of an underrepresented community and the progress that powerful women aviators make each year toward representation and equality, all while having some good old flying fun.

It's events like these that truly get the excitement for aviation going—the roar of aircraft engines, the deep rumble of turboprops, the shiny and colorful airplanes that dip and soar through the sky. It's also events like these that encourage and motivate prospective women pilots and pilots of color to get into the cockpit and envision themselves there. These airshows, aviation education days, and aviation advocacy events allow our future pilots to see themselves up in the clouds in the future, all under the disguise of some classic, exciting fun.

INTERESTED IN THE EAA?

None of the excitement and motivation that Oshkosh inspires would be possible without the EAA. There are ways for you to get involved as well. For anyone interested, head to EAA.org online, and find a flight chapter near you! If they don't have one, start one—you won't regret it. If you're interested in a Young Eagle's program and taking your first discovery flight, ask your local chapter as well: the EAA provides insurance and helps with organization of these events, making it easier than ever to share the spirit of aviation. As Sarah says, "The EAA wants to see everyone fly—all you need is a love of flight!"

CHAPTER 5

AVIATION EDUCATION

———

The past few years have given rise to a new way to get into aviation. Reserved for those that have absolute confidence in their passion for flight, aviation academies provide a relatively cost-efficient method to get from zero previous flight training all the way to becoming a commercial pilot, and fast. In just nine months, and for the average cost of a year's college tuition, dedicated pilots graduate from these academies ready to enter the workforce.

BRAVEEN & AVIATION ACADEMIES

When I first met with Braveen Mahendran, a helicopter tour pilot in New York, we discussed his personal path through aviation. As a young glider pilot in Oregon state, Braveen decided that his future belonged in the skies. He knew that the traditional nine-to-five desk job was not something he wanted to endure. With that said, he also knew that unless he wanted to end up in that position, he would have to set out and do something about it. Within the year, Braveen had signed up with Hillsboro Aero Academy and was on track to get his helicopter licenses.

Transitioning from the mechanics of gliding to the intricacies of rotorcraft wasn't easy. As with any training, it required a significant amount of determination to get through. He recalls:

Flying on the strict schedule I was given absolutely made me a better pilot. It made sure that I developed as a person as well, because it forced me to have the discipline to follow through on my goals, even when it was tough to do so. I went from not studying for the past three years to having to study every single day. That was not easy, and if I didn't have the push from the academy, I don't think I would've been able to actually get to where I am today.

The regimented schedule of a dedicated flight school such as Hillsboro Aero Academy, while strict, is a great way to ensure that student pilots accomplish what they set out to do. It ensures that trainees work through their flight problems, rather than putting them off. It also minimizes any plateaus that may come up in training, as students are expected to fly at least every other day.

I think that most of the obstacles in flying are good obstacles. It's classic learning—you make mistakes, and then you fix them. Over and over, until they are committed to memory. Not to mention the resources that the Academy has, you always have people around that you can ask for help. And the full-time aspect of the academy is great: I would be learning something on the ground one day and practicing it in the air the next. Pretty intense, but I got my certificates super fast and was able to start teaching people how to do the thing that I love.

The benefits of having a community of peers all passionate about flying is arguably one of the best resources that a flight school could have. The ability to get the help you need when you need it is a huge part of being able to work past any setbacks that you may have as a pilot-in-training and in life itself. Not to mention, it makes actually learning the material much more fun than it is otherwise.

Another thing that Braveen covered in our talks was the importance of learning to fly when you are younger:

> Remember, you're not only learning to fly, you're taking in all this new knowledge about aviation and FAA laws. And this isn't just with aviation, but in general: you learn better when you're younger. I guess your brain just works a little faster when you're young, because I've seen firsthand the difference in proficiency between my seventeen-year-old pilots and my forty-year-old students.

The way that Braveen sees it, aviation will always come with its costs. However, based on his personal experience, reaching out to those young potential pilots is the very best way that our industry stays alive. No matter what the affordability of flight is, those that are determined to fly will—and the introduction of these modernized academies can and will play a large part in that story.

THE STORY OF RAISBECK AVIATION HIGH SCHOOL
The sky is *not* the limit. At least, not for students at Raisbeck Aviation High School. As mentioned in the beginning of this book, this unique place serves as the teaching grounds for

hundreds of students—an aviation and aerospace-themed STEM college preparatory school serving the diverse public school district of Highline. A quick Google search will bring you to the school's webpage, as well as the Wikipedia page, where you can view all the really cool and unique things that RAHS itself offers. For those of you interested in applying, don't worry about cost—it's a public school!

Founded by Principal Reba Gilman, the school was originally dubbed Aviation High School and came to fruition in 2004. The idea for an aviation-themed high school initially started forming as a result of Ms. Gilman's work at the Puget Sound Skill Center (PSSC). As she spoke with the ambitious and underserved students that went through the program, a common theme began to emerge: these kids wanted to pursue more in the field of aviation. They wanted to be astronauts and engineers; they wanted to be pilots and aviation technicians; and, perhaps most importantly, they didn't want to have to wait until college to do so. As a result, the PSSC began courses in these topics for upperclassmen.

There was only one small problem: students would come excited about the prospect of flight but didn't always follow through the intense workload that came with trying to enter the industry that late in their high school careers. The solution? Start them earlier. Get them excited to begin learning about aerospace and aviation at a younger age so they don't have to cram years worth of knowledge into a couple semesters of learning. And so, the Aviation High School was born.

After a couple rounds of community advocacy, the project began to really take shape. At the beginning, the school was a shot in the dark. The students went to class on the campus of South Seattle Community College for the first three years. Once additional funding came through, the dedicated staff and faculty "upgraded" to an abandoned middle school— lovingly known by current students as "Old Aviation." After getting the water leaks fixed and the old school mostly functioning, heavy support came through from private as well as corporate donors: the Boeing Company, Alaska Airlines, Esterline, and Dr. James Raisbeck of Raisbeck Engineering.

Passionate about the school's mission, Dr. Raisbeck was the first investor in the school. He not only stirred up support, but he also donated, in layman's terms, a *lot* of money. This was funding that would provide the staff of Aviation High School with a brand-new facility, state-of-the-art technology, and up close and personal access to the Pacific Northwest's aviation giants. The new Raisbeck Aviation High School opened its doors in 2013 on the campus of our local Museum of Flight, located directly next to Boeing's Seattle factories—which of course are next to the Boeing Field International Airport. Walk into the lobby, look up, and there are experimental airfoils and student-built aircraft hanging from the ceiling, as well as countless awards and banners lining the walls. Perhaps the most distinguishable feature of the new facility, though, was the direct access to the Museum of Flight resources. If you take a glance out of the massive windows, you'll see dozens of historical aircraft including Air Force One and Concorde, which are open to students to tour for free.

Access to Raisbeck Aviation wasn't easy though. In previous years, the school had an intensive application process.

Students previously had to go through a twelve-page application and then a ninety-minute interview with school faculty and current students—of which only 30 percent of students were accepted. These days, a lottery process is now in place: students that have an expressed interest in aviation and aerospace are now selected for admission through drawing, although the application remains in place. For those that are interested and didn't receive an offer of admission, don't worry. The Museum of Flight offers something just as good—a Washington Aerospace Scholars department, which gives high school students college credit for attendance of their aviation-based programs.

As I write this story, RAHS is ranked as Washington's number two public high school. A good chunk of this can be attributed to the new technology and learning resources that are offered to the "plane gang," but the school was earning awards long before it ever received all of that recognition. We've received distinguishable mentions and secured a huge community backing. Aviation literally operates in our backyard. Why is this? Pure passion—and, of course, money and community support.

Students come to this school to jump headfirst into the aviation industry, to get their hands dirty working on aircraft, and to take courses that will propel them into the world of aviation, aerospace, and STEM. Our teachers also all have a general connection to the world of flight. Many of them were pilots themselves, or Boeing Engineers, or Museum of Flight volunteers. All of that passion and dedication lends itself exceptionally well to the mission of the school: "To prepare all students for college, career, and citizenship through a personalized, rigorous, and relevant learning experience that is facilitated in the context of aviation and aerospace."

As with any school, RAHS had its own issues. There is a cap to the number of accepted students. However—and I may be biased—the school itself has the most unique and innovative approach to learning about aerospace that I have seen thus far. In addition to their standardized school work (think state and College Board exams) and extracurriculars (robotics, speech and debate, Science Olympiad, solar car, and space satellite team), students have a rigorous program that overall lends itself very well to preparing students for a career in aviation and STEM.

This is known as our career readiness program, and I think it is the most valuable experience at RAHS. Students are paired up with a mentor in the field of aviation/aerospace depending on their interests. For example, students interested in aviation might get assigned a mentor from Boeing while students wanting to head into aerospace would receive a mentor from Blue Origin. These mentors serve as a guide throughout the student's high school career and help prepare them for interviews, get them ready to network with professionals in the industry, and are an overall pillar of support as the students progress through high school. To best make their mark on the world, students receive access to the Museum of Flight, galas and black-tie dinner events, and unique aviation internships—all for free. Due to events like the Pathfinder Gala (which celebrates notable figures in aviation and aerospace) and exclusive access to Boeing internships, our students are ready to jump directly into aviation and higher education immediately after graduation—knocking down many of the obstacles that stood in our path.

AVIATION FUNDAMENTALS: BEGIN WITH A QUALITY EDUCATION

Of course, if you're reading this book, you're probably interested in the pilot side of things as well. One of the reasons that I was able to keep my flight training costs so low was that I had opportunities to learn to fly for free from school alumni and teachers. In other words, a major chunk of my flight costs disappeared due to my instructors' willingness to support the students of the school. I also was fortunate enough to earn a fantastic scholarship from the Museum of Flight, which paid for the rest. Being right next to a major airport also helps. Local flight schools often gave RAHS students discounts on their training, and the location was very effective—I would drive five minutes after school to the airport and immediately begin my lessons.

Getting an education at Raisbeck Aviation didn't just mean running to the windows every time a loud fighter jet took off. It meant sharing our parking lot with a 747 and driving underneath the wing of a retired B-52 bomber. As self-respecting high school students, we often made jokes about our affinity for airplanes, dubbing ourselves the "Plane Gang." And yet, despite our nerdy reputation, having the airplanes sit right outside our classrooms and hearing the roar of jet turbines overhead gave us a constant reminder that we were in fact living in our very own world of flight and that we were proud to do so.

Evidently, RAHS was and still is a very successful story of aviation advocacy. If you give young and prospective students the opportunity to explore their dreams and place them in a position where they can envision themselves being successful by pursuing those dreams, you get a very straightforward result: students will follow their dreams. We ended up being unafraid to enter this world of flight, primarily because we were surrounded by it. We lived and breathed it. We heard it outside our windows, saw it outside our windows, and connected to it outside our windows. If there was ever such a thing as too much aviation, we probably had it. The problem, then, became getting it out to a wider audience.

With only one hundred seats per class, the community of Raisbeck Aviation High School was naturally selective. However, the lessons that we can draw from it are not—we know that advocacy works and that it works extremely well. Taking that idea and introducing it to the public as a whole, creating a larger scale Aviation High School—that should be the goal of aviation right now. When you place young and prospective students into the pilot's seat of an aircraft, when you walk them through the complicated process of getting into the aviation and aerospace industry, and when you not only show them role models but allow them to connect and interact with those models, it all reinforces the idea that they can pursue this aviation dream of theirs. That is exactly when you begin getting results. If we as an industry want our numbers to grow, that is how we do it. Aviation education is the absolute very first step to lowering the barriers of entry for our hobbies and careers above the clouds, and without them, it will always be difficult to get people interested in the wonders of flight. These programs get young people inspired to take the first step and dip their toes into the world of flight. Participating in aviation programs—even small ones—opens the door for people to take the first step, as it presents them with the opportunity to experience the fun of flight for themselves.

MATT AND THE MUSEUM OF FLIGHT

Opportunities to promote aviation and aerospace exist away from the airport as well. I mentioned earlier the amazing resources that being on the campus of the Museum of Flight (MoF) offered RAHS students like myself. In fact, many of our projects and volunteer opportunities were in partnership with the museum next door, seeing as we had unlimited access to the diverse and incredible knowledge that was just outside our windows. Sure, the museum itself offered an admittedly envy-inducing view of historical and famous aircraft, but more than that, it offered the best selection of aviation advocacy you could find.

As it stands, the Museum of Flight is the largest independent nonprofit air and space museum in the world, with a collection of over 175 air and spacecraft. Originating from a small group of aviation enthusiasts dubbing themselves the Pacific Northwest Aviation Historical Foundation, the first aviation artifacts went on exhibit in 1965. The Museum of Flight truly found its home, however, when the Boeing Red Barn—the birthplace of a small international Fortune 500 company that you may have heard about—was leased to the museum by the Port of Seattle. The old building was saved from demolition and restored in 1983 and was the very first permanent location for the MoF. As more and more enthusiasts donated their money and aircraft, the museum expanded rapidly, joined by even bigger and more modern buildings. Today, it boasts dozens of eye-catching and informative exhibits as well as a world-class library.

The mission of the MoF is clear. In fact, it says it right on their website: "The Museum of Flight exists to acquire, preserve, and exhibit historically significant air and space artifacts, which provide a foundation for scholarly research and lifelong learning programs that inspire an interest in and understanding of science, technology, and the humanities." In other words, they want more students to envision themselves in a role at the crossroads of STEM and aviation. They want more students to view aviation as a viable path, to know about it as a valuable option—and they want to be the organization that helps make it happen.

That was all stuff that you could've gotten online, however, and this book is supposed to give you insights on not just how to become a pilot, but why these programs are essential to transforming the industry. For that, I reached out to Matt Hayes, the current CEO of the Museum of Flight, for an interview.

Matt got his start in the world of aviation as a student in rural New York. As he read captivating stories about pilots and their role in society, he wanted to get his own start in the industry—originally wishing to fly the crop duster planes that he saw crisscrossing the sky each day. His parents, thinking it was just a phase, eventually gave in and signed him up for a discovery flight so that Matt could "get it out of his system." Needless to say, it didn't exactly work out that way, and Matt put himself through three different jobs. As he tells it, "One was for college, one was for my flying lessons, and the other was for my car and my gas." He eventually achieved his pilot's license at seventeen.

As Matt grew up, his career path changed slightly, but eventually his love of flight landed him a volunteer position on a B-17 restoration project with the Museum of Flight. As the project came to a close, he stayed involved because of the educational mission as well as the incredible people that were just as involved in aviation as he was. He began spending more and more time with the museum and quickly found himself at the front of the line for an open position as CEO, which he happily accepted.

For Matt specifically, the educational mission of the MoF is the biggest priority today, and the collection and preservation of aviation history plays a massive role in that. He views their role as a museum in providing the connection between the industry and the curious minds of students and applies that inspirational approach to the museum's aviation education programs.

As such, Matt ensured that the Museum of Flight offered curious and passionate students the chance to get involved in the world of aviation through his ASP project.

THE PATH TO A GREAT EDUCATION

The Aeronautical Science Pathway (ASP) offers a unique opportunity for high school students in the state of Washington. By partnering with aviation and aerospace departments at local colleges, the program presents a college level curriculum (and the opportunity to receive inexpensive college credits) as a true introduction to the world of flight. It provides them with advanced coursework and the opportunity to connect and network with prominent figures in aviation in preparation for these bright young minds to enter and propel the aviation industry forward. Essentially, the program is "real-world experience to go with the practical application of flight," and has the added benefit of college credits to give these students an edge in their higher education goals.

By providing the next generation of pilots and aviation enthusiasts with an opportunity to get involved with the aviation industry early on, ASP allows students to see themselves in this unique world. It also does the same for the other side: it allows potential employers to see the incredible interest and new ideas that these innovators are able to bring to the table. It fosters creativity and passion in order to accelerate the world of aviation into the modern age and a modern way of thinking. It's exactly the type of program we need more of to get more students into the cockpit and into the air.

The Museum of Flight, as Matt proudly points out, doesn't just offer ASP either. They also offer additional specialized programs, such as the Western Aerospace Scholars (WAS), which focuses on the space exploration side of things. Offered to students from Washington, Oregon, and Montana, these prospective high school juniors have the ability to participate in a seven-week project involving NASA's space exploration program, with the opportunity to become a resident in a weeklong research project with NASA scientists—and earning them access to a strong alumni network of 1600 students at top colleges and companies across the United States.

Let's say that you want to start even younger than high school. For that, the MoF offers ACE: Aerospace Camp Experience (much like the world of flight, the Museum of Flight loves its acronyms). At this day camp, younger students are given the opportunity to explore the museum itself and are given activities related to aeronautics and aerospace to get them thinking about the science behind it all. While it may sound cheesy, camps like these are essential to inspiring young minds: students are much more likely to enter the aviation industry if they are given the chance to envision themselves in it from a young age. Matt refers to this process as "vegetables in the ice cream," which, he admits, does sound terrible, but it gets the point across. By hiding "boring" aerospace education in the bounds of fun interactive experiments, these young pilots get to genuinely learn about the world around them and see themselves doing this in the future. This then inspires many to pursue aviation and STEM career paths.

In short, the Museum of Flight and other organizations like it are essential to the aviation industry. The programs they offer put flying in the minds of students from a very young age, showing them that they have the opportunity to follow such a career path. Matt is a huge supporter of that, especially as he adapts the museum to a modern way of teaching. With such a wealth of resources in his backyard, his programs are able to show firsthand the excitement of flight and give students the chance to learn about and find their own futures in the world above the clouds. To those that can see this flying life at the forefront of their imaginations, he has a few simple words: "Find a way, find a museum, and keep your head in the clouds."

MUSEUM OF FLIGHT

Are you interested in the Museum of Flight? Feel free to head directly to their website for a virtual tour of the exhibits. Recently, with an uptick in vaccinations, the museum has also been able to take visitors in person! As one of the largest nonprofit aviation museums in the world, the museum offers countless artifacts, models, and wonderful volunteers who are more than happy to recall their stories in aviation. Keep an eye out for cool events, such as new exhibit displays, as well as the unique aviation pavilion.

CHAPTER 6

DIVERSITY PROGRAMS AND EDUCATION

We know about the benefits of diversity—they've been clearly laid out for us in study after study. Just like any other industry, the aviation world would benefit from having the unique and interesting perspectives that underrepresented pilots bring to the table. New ideas, fresh ideas—these lead to advancement and evolution in our system, and advancement and evolution quite often lead to more proficient and safe pilots, not to mention more pilots overall.

Resources for connecting with underrepresented pilots include collegiate aeronautical science programs, the FAA's Educational Partnership Initiative, and specialized programs such as the Black Pilots Association (BPA), the Organization of Black Aerospace Professionals (OBAP), Women in Aviation International (WAI), the Professional Asian Pilots Association (PAPA), and the National Gay Pilots Association (NGPA). These groups are essential to the diversification movement within aviation—advocating for diversity and growth as well as breaking the stereotype of the white, male pilot.

As such, these programs all specialize in a couple of common goals: to show underrepresented minorities that they do have a place in the cockpit and that they do have role models in the field. I will tell you that as a young Asian pilot, it always inspired me to be able to talk to another Asian pilot. The sole factor of being able to see that there were others like me in the tight-knit world of aviation gave me a special boost, a collaborative uplifting mindset to continue pushing toward my flying goals. This representation is necessary to foster a sense of belonging. Particularly for groups that experience the daily prejudices of society, having a role model that looks like you is a bigger boost than you might think. As the saying goes, it's one thing to tell people that they can do it and another to show them that they can do it.

JESSE HAYES AND THE RED-TAILED HAWKS PROGRAM

Over the summer, I was given the unique opportunity to sit down and have a chat with Jesse Hayes, the founder of the Red-Tailed Hawks. The Red-Tailed Hawks are a fantastic organization within the Seattle area that promote the concept and reality of flight for the next generation of pilots of color. In fact, I was able to see the organization operate firsthand at their annual aviation day—a fantastic opportunity for young and underrepresented prospective pilots to get behind the wheel of an airplane.

As I walked out onto the ramp area of their flight operations at Boeing Field, it was clear that the Hawks knew what they were doing. Campers went through a very specific process: they gave their presentations to one another on the physics of flight and earth sciences and then were given the opportunity to apply their new aviation knowledge in the cockpit.

As I got to know the younger pilots and engineers-to-be, they told me about how much of an impact the program genuinely had upon them.

"The club showed me everything about flying—things that I couldn't get from the classroom. They put me in a plane and showed me how fun it is to fly and showed me that I could actually become a pilot."

"I know a lot more about how to get my license, and I can really see myself flying one day. I'm actually going to college at [a local aviation college] to get my degree in aviation science."

"This program helped me learn about more than just flying. I learned all about the airplane, how it flies, how it works. It's not a mystery anymore."

These students were great at what they did and knew just how far they wanted to take their flying careers, primarily because they were given a clear opportunity to learn, unburdened by extreme costs. As I spoke with some of them, it was clear they were happy to be here—engaged in socially distanced classrooms, they continued to have fun with their friends and learned all they could about the science and history behind what made airplanes fly. It was clear to me that I was talking with those who would be our future ambitious pilots, engineers, and technicians.

As flight operations began, the students were called out onto the active aviation ramp. A mix of general aviation airplanes and helicopters had landed and rolled in to assist with the discovery flight–style activity. Groups of three walked out to the planes and began boarding. They would take off and fly toward downtown Seattle, given an opportunity to ask questions and to briefly take the controls and then turn back and come in for a landing.

Equipped with a detailed in-flight worksheet, the students were tasked with learning all that they could about the flight. In doing so, the young Red-Tailed Hawks were able to decide for themselves whether flying was something that they truly wanted to do.

In Jesse's own words, "I won't let these kids not go into aviation because it was something they didn't genuinely know about. They can choose to do whatever they want, but it's not right to leave them in the dark about a potential dream they have." And the campers would agree—while all of them came back with a smile, most came back beaming, excited for their futures as pilots and engineers. No matter what they would decide to do, they were given the opportunity to see what could be—and that is the most important part of ushering in the next generation of pilots.

Jesse's approach to the group was largely built off of his own experiences. Introduced to the world of flight by a local aviation club, Jesse was able to power through and complete his first solo at age fifteen. Raised in a military family, Jesse attended and graduated from the United States Air Force Academy in 1985 with a degree in aeronautical engineering.

From there, he decided to continue his passion for flight in the United States Air Force, earning the rank of major and logging over 3,300 hours in military C-130s, including 150 in combat during the Gulf War.

Jesse credits the military for teaching him how to fly—and for teaching him how to deal with racism in the cockpit. It also demonstrated to him the need for Black aviators to have strong role models in the sky. "My parents had kept me pretty sheltered while I grew up, so I didn't really see the whole racism thing until I left home....From there, I had to deal with a lot of racists. People who hated that I outranked them, who hated that I could achieve anything in my career. I remember there was this one instructor that refused to pass me—I actually had to fly with my CO himself to show that I wasn't, you know, a garbage pilot. He told me afterwards it was the best ride he'd ever done—and I was finally able to get signed off." With that story fresh in mind, Jesse was determined to help others like him reach new heights.

As we spoke, Jesse reminisced about his days in the Air Force. Despite the adversity he faced, he emphasized that it was a great program and that there were a lot of good people that did want to see him succeed. He also emphasized one of the chief benefits that the military provided him with: a clear cut way into the cockpit of some of the world's most powerful aircraft. Jesse's patriotism made the USAF a clear path forward for him, seeing as he was able to get all of his necessary licenses through his service. He cautions against joining for the free training though: "I would say that you never should sign up for the military just to get your flight training done—that's just not a smart decision. There's other ways to do that. However, I made it clear to my kids that I would be proud if they signed up for the military to serve their country and did so as a pilot."

While he was in the Air Force, Jesse helped start a new chapter of the Black Pilots of America: the Arkansas Thunderbirds. Heavily involved with the general aviation community, he promoted diversity and a passion for flight throughout that club and then went on to establish more and more. "Once I realized that people that looked like me were dealing with all this prejudice even in the cockpit, that was when I decided I had to do something about it—there shouldn't be anything holding them back from pursuing their dreams." In Waco, Texas, Jesse started the Bronze Eagles Flying Club's Waco Chapter, giving back to the very club that allowed him that first taste of flight. To further connect with the community and have some good old aviation fun, Jesse also began the annual tradition of the Waco Youth Fly-In, giving young pilots the opportunity to connect through their love of flight.

As mentioned before, Jesse's passion project is the Red-Tailed Hawks. Once he moved to Washington state, he started the program with a clear mission in mind: to provide underserved and underrepresented youth an opportunity to learn about the world of flight. The Learn to Fly program is emphasized the most—young prospective pilots who express a clear and strong desire to genuinely fly are able to earn scholarships to the BPA's Summer Flight Academy as well as the Red-Tailed Hawks' very own FLY program. By completing coursework based on lesson plans straight out of the FAA's Pilot's Handbook of Aeronautical Knowledge (PHAK) and actively participating in the club, these next-generation pilots are able to secure themselves enough training for their first solo—and for a greatly reduced price as well, further knocking down the barriers to entry.

With this mission in mind, the Red-Tailed Hawks program has grown greatly within the Pacific Northwest. Local sponsors include Lockheed Martin, the Museum of Flight, Alaska Airlines, and many local flight-based organizations. A large grant donation by the Boeing Employees' Credit Union allowed the Hawks to buy their very own Cessna 172 aircraft, and it recently landed in the Pacific Northwest in May of 2021, with more on the way. Not only did the aircraft provide students with the chance to gain flight experience, it also gave them a chance to genuinely visualize what they were learning about in the classroom.

Throughout our talks, Jesse made it clear that he is passionate about continuing the group's growth and impact. "The reality is that people go after the things that they know, not the things that they don't know about. Especially for Black folks, who are given an expectation to do certain things and not other things, like flying. That's exactly why we need to keep going, because I don't want these kids to miss out on the joys of flying because they just don't know about it."

For many prospective minority pilots, flying can seem out of reach. It isn't hard to see why: it's difficult to see yourself in a position when there aren't many role models to follow. Diversity is an area in which aviation has struggled for a long time, and it wouldn't be a very good book on the next generation of pilots if I didn't speak to the great things that current pilots are attempting to do for the field. It is through these diversity and advocacy programs like Jesse Hayes's Red-Tailed Hawks that minority pilots and pilots from underserved communities have a chance to envision themselves in the cockpit. When you provide students with a path to success, you'll find a lot more begin taking that road—and that's where we want to be.

WANT TO SUPPORT THE RED-TAILED HAWKS?

Head online to redtailedhawksflyingclub.org where you can find a full list of services they provide, as well as blog posts and videos about what they do and who they are. As a 501(c)3 organization, all donations are tax-deductible and are dedicated to their mission of providing local youth the opportunity to get into the air.

CHAPTER 7

HOW PILOTS ARE MAKING AVIATION MORE ACCESSIBLE

———

JACK GAVIN'S STORY

We often hear the phrase "giving back to the community." The issue is not everyone knows how. That isn't a problem for Jack Gavin, an ambitious student with one goal in mind: making sure that others have the opportunity to get their heads in the clouds.

Jack's path to obtaining his Private Pilot License (PPL) was, in his words, "a lot of twists and turns." None of his family had active ties to aviation: the last pilot was his great-grandfather, and even then, there wasn't much flying going on. It actually wasn't until his parents won a local airplane ride that Jack knew he was interested in the word of flight. Shortly afterwards, Jack found himself drawn to the small airport near his house, where he would sit and watch countless aircraft take off and land for hours on end. Eventually, he decided to get closer to the action and began to volunteer his time at the local Experimental Aviation Association chapter on the field.

For many students across the country, opportunities like this are essential to getting them ready for takeoff. Discovery flights, such as the one that Jack was able to participate in, offer an entirely new experience for students that might never have been interested in flying otherwise.

Additionally, because a local EAA chapter existed near his home, Jack was able to get involved in the heat of the action. Clubs such as these offer more than an opportunity to get close to aircraft; they offer the chance to meet others in the aviation community. Pancake breakfasts, fly-ins, and aviation camps all bring pilots together for community events that keep everyone connected. According to a 2011 study by the Airplane Owners and Pilots Association, or AOPA, 71 percent of pilots stated that one of their favorable aspect of training was the friendliness of their instructors and classmates, and 61 percent of pilots stated another favorable aspect was being a part of a tight-knit aviation community.

With all the hours Jack spent working with the EAA program, he was offered a great opportunity. Pretty soon, Jack was on a single engine plane, tagging along on a flight with some local chapter pilots down to the heart of aviation: Oshkosh AirVenture. It was on that trip that he knew for sure that aviation was his future.

However, achieving his goal was much easier said than done. To truly pursue his dream of flight, he needed to first be able to *afford* his dream of flight. How exactly that would happen,

Jack wasn't sure. But his countless hours spent at the airport opened his door to opportunity: a potential scholarship to help him achieve his goals.

I was lucky enough to be on that trip to Oshkosh, and I was lucky enough to realize on that trip that this was what I wanted to do with my life. Even if I couldn't afford to become a pilot, I can become a mechanic, I can work with these planes and this community—either way, I knew I was going to be working with planes.

It was that mindset that got Jack's face recognized at the Young Eagles program, and the local EAA chapter came to the rescue, providing him with the scholarship that he needed to make his dream a possibility. A recent sponsor presented the chapter with a great opportunity: an offer of ten grand, available to Jack to complete his training. There was a stipulation in the prize money, though—a catch that required Jack to fly at least three times a week while he worked toward his license.

It was that catch, though, that ensured Jack would follow through on his goals.

That scholarship gave me what I needed to pull through: I had the motivation to fly, now I had the money. In addition to that, I had the extra push of having to fly three days a week—no matter what, I would be in the air, applying what I learned. I would say that was the biggest motivator of all; even when I was feeling overwhelmed, I knew I had to get myself up into the sky. That was really the key—that gave me the discipline I needed to take on that one short field landing I was struggling with or cleaning up my stalls so that I could fly it to near perfection.

Jack brings up a great point here: flying, although 100 percent worth it in the end, is no easy task, and it's easy to reach a plateau. Any pilot will tell you that there are flights that make you want to throw in the towel. Maybe you just couldn't nail that landing, or maybe you had an especially harsh air traffic controller speaking to you. Either way, the only way to get past that slump is to get right back into the air and follow through on what you've learned.

In fact, many instructors (including my own and others from popular flight schools in the Ann Arbor, MI, and Seattle, WA, region) recommend a two day per week *minimum* when you first begin to fly. "Flying," they say, especially when you first learn it, "is a very 'use it or lose it' skill set." As a benchmark, flight schools with dedicated private pilot training programs such as ATP or Sling Aviation Academy estimate a three-month timeline from zero hours to completion if you fly about two to three times a week. For pilots that only flew once or twice a month, that timeline could increase to six to twelve months. In a way, it was that catch of needing to fly three times a week that ensured Jack would have the discipline to get through his obstacles.

As a young pilot, Jack is part of the population that will dictate how the future of general aviation will evolve, and he loves every second of his journey:

There is nothing better than being able to wake up one morning and say—you know what? I'm going to go fly today. That alone is worth all the roadblocks I had to go through.

However, having recently gone through the process, Jack mentions there are definitely ways to tackle training and make it easier for future pilots to take control.

Honestly, if we can get this thing to be cheaper, that tackles the biggest issue right there. As student pilots, we not only pay a couple hundred for the plane, but then we need to pay a good chunk of money to our instructors as well. And I'm not saying they don't deserve it, but there needs to be a more efficient way of accomplishing this. If we can't get aviation to be cheaper, this industry can quickly begin to decline.

What Jack brings up here is pretty much a common theme across the industry. Out of the countless Facebook and Instagram surveys I've conducted, most pilots—whether they have ten hours or five thousand—agree that reducing the barrier to entry (in this case, cost) will allow general aviation to continue and even grow. Of course, it makes sense. Having to cough up ten thousand dollars just to get your license is a great way to prevent optimistic young pilots from following their dreams. That cost is increasing, and if it continues to climb, the general aviation industry will only remain stagnant.

To his credit, Jack and his family have already taken steps to allow others to pursue their dream. Realizing that he had a privilege that many others don't receive through his scholarship, he set out to truly "give back to the community."

It all started with this pandemic. Great start to a great story, I know. Anyway, a small PSI testing center shut down since they couldn't sustain their operations, and that left a lot of students out in the cold. So I saw a nice opportunity to jump in and follow through on my goal, you know, the affordable flight school. My family and I ended up buying the place, a nice FBO on the airport, and getting it set up again as a testing site. I didn't want to stop there though, and so we're slowly getting the flight-training portion of it set up. I started thinking, what would I want to train in as a student? I would want a reliable, stable airplane, and I immediately arrived at the Cessna series. We found a relatively inexpensive C-172, and while it currently serves as my personal plane, we've been getting it ready for flight training. So as of right now, our main source of revenue is from the testing services, but eventually we'll open the flight portion of the school, begin hiring instructors as independent contract pilots, and expand our operations while continuing to provide cheaper instruction and aircraft rental than your traditional flight school.

Jack's method works, too: many low-key flight clubs operate using this structure. From what I've seen, they offer the most affordable prices around. Find one that suits your needs, and you often find yourself saving a significant amount of money (in the thousands) on flight training. Jack also addresses another topic in his thoughts on general aviation, though, and it's one that I think is important.

The goal is to make flying more accessible to the general public, and we typically just look at the ways that we can get people into airplanes. But what we often leave out is the airports. Most of our airports are publicly funded, and yet a very small fraction of those citizens ever get to use them. If we really want general aviation to stick around, we need the public support of the communities around the airport—and we do that by offering events, camps, and other things that truly get those citizens involved. Right now, general aviation is more of a hidden gem, and if we want it to keep going, we need to spread our message. A great way to do that is through these local airports.

The idea that Jack is bringing up here is commonly overlooked: most aviation events at airfields are primarily for pilots. I'm not saying that's a bad thing, but if we truly want to expand our industry, more and more events should be geared toward youth. It will be the natural curiosity of children that constantly adds to our currently exclusive aviation ranks, and there is no better way to pique curiosity than by having children play around with machines that fly.

Jack's story has all the makings of a classic struggle, but it's his perseverance that pulled him through in the end. Jack knows how local aviation camps and programs genuinely work and why they're so important for getting youth interested in the world of flight. The point of flight isn't to keep it to ourselves, but to share it with others so they can experience the fun of flying and see what we get to see.

DAVID TUSHIN AND CHECKRIDE PREP

Doing a quick Google search of "how to become a pilot" offers up a *long* list of ways to become a pilot. These range from local aviation programs to the Civil Air Patrol and the EAA Young Eagles. Regardless of their size, these programs have one thing in common: they expose young potential pilots to flight. Whether it is offering flight time or the chance to get your glider license, these programs take your average kid and present them with the opportunity to get behind the wheel of an airplane. And what better way to gather interest than by letting a young, inexperienced child operate a real machine?

Just about everything in the aviation world circles back to a primary issue: money. Being one of the most expensive hobbies in the world is certainly not without its drawbacks, and the setbacks are visible in just about every aviation group you ask. As a result, the best way to reduce the barriers to entry? Find a way to make things cheaper.

Enter Checkride Prep, LLC. Started by David Tushin back in 2017, Checkride Prep was his way to share his love of flight with a great community. The Camarillo, California-based flight school quickly grew, expanding with each year that passed—right up until the COVID-19 pandemic that has devastated the country. David, passionate about continuing to grow his business and seeing the inequities that coronavirus caused, decided to do something practically unheard of within the aviation industry: offer a free, online ground school for private pilots all the way up to commercial pilots.

To give an idea of how fundamentally special this program is, an in-person private pilot ground school can cost upwards of five hundred dollars. By providing this service for free, students are able to better focus on learning the material, not how light their wallets feel. The virtual program also has another advantage. Ground schools are normally in person, meaning that interested students must take time out of their day to drive out to their local flight school for training.

Obviously, that doesn't always work out: students have school or a lack of transportation, or they simply don't want to drive longer distances. With Checkride Prep, that issue no longer exists. Switching to this virtual format may have its negatives, but the ability to have a remote, free course is worth its weight in gold.

Full disclosure: I received both my Instrument and my Commercial Written endorsements from Checkride Prep, and the process went pretty well, especially for a class size of over one thousand students at its peak. I was so impressed with the process that I reached out to David himself for an interview—a free online ground school is capable of saving students hundreds of dollars in their training, a feat that very obviously meets the requirements of lowering the barriers to entry of flight.

* * *

Starting to fly in his college years, David was split on what to do. He spent half of his time on campus and the other half at the airport trying to complete his Private Pilot License. This was back in 2001, which was not a great year for aviation: 9/11 had sent pilot demand plummeting into what the aviation industry calls the lost generation of pilots. Pilots who were excited and ready to enter a booming industry were now finding it exceptionally hard to find jobs, stuck in smaller and lower-paying roles for a much longer time period. As the decade continued, though, demand for pilots began to rise once more and to record levels—piloting was once again offered a livable wage.

By that point in time, David, who was working a desk job, was ready to try an innovative way to break into the field. Watching some aviation influencers on YouTube and seeing their journey as they went from their first solo to receiving their Airline Transport Pilot's License inspired him to continue forward with his aviation career. The rise of the internet had given many a look into the previously hidden world of flight, and David was hooked.

Rather than sit bored at a desk all day, David wanted to fly. He studied hard, and began to teach others. Receiving his ground instruction certificate, he began to teach pilot ground schools to help pay for the new flight bills, not only developing his own knowledge but getting him to the point where he was eligible to become a flight instructor. As a result, David committed fully to the world of flight in 2017, starting Checkride Prep after receiving his CFI license.

While the flight school did well for the first couple of years, the pandemic brought many things to a halt—and that's when some students of David suggested starting an online ground school. While online ground schools had been around for years, none of them had ever been truly organized before. As a result, when Checkride Prep first posted about this opportunity on Facebook, the program exploded. "We put an ad out on Facebook, and I want to say Monday morning we suddenly had three thousand, maybe four thousand people in class." It turns out that a lot of people want to fly, and this was the perfect way to introduce them to that world.

That makes sense, too—I was astonished when I first learned about the opportunity. As a pilot debating about going for my instrument rating (I am happy to say I am now instrument rated), Checkride Prep's free Instrument Ground School was the primary catalyst. If I hadn't come across the post on Facebook, I'm not sure I would've started the training as early as I did. That seems to check out for a lot of others, too:

"I started doing private pilot one-on-ones for these private pilots that were beginning to fall behind. What I found was you can get people excited because this isn't something that they were sure that they wanted to do at first—and I've met people who say, 'Hey I took your class, and I didn't even know the first thing about [aviation],' but they still sign up and they still want to enter that world."

It is that ability to satisfy curiosity that truly promotes the next generation of pilots. In my opinion, the best thing about these classes is that they provide prospective pilots of all different backgrounds a free, in-depth look at the flying world. It's just like David says—these are people that were curious about aviation at one point in time or another, and it's thanks to the removal of the barriers to entry that they can finally see what they've been missing. You have not only young students ranging from the age of seven to twenty-five, but you also have older folks that were always curious about this world and never got the chance to explore it, all coming together and bonding over their interest in aviation. That point is also heavily emphasized throughout the groups that have sprung up with student pilots to help one another make it through the intensity of ground school.

As I asked fellow classmates about their thoughts, many revealed to me that the private pilot ground school course

David offered served as a huge reminder of this dream they had not so long ago and that taking the class was the first step in realizing that goal once more. Imagine if the barriers to entry had been lowered for them years ago—would they be part of the aviation world we see today?

I served as a moderator for these online courses and got to see the diversity of the course as represented in the Facebook study groups. It was easily the most diverse group of pilots I had ever seen anywhere in aviation. The numbers were impressive, too: peak attendance easily soared above one thousand people, all of them there to take the first step into the world of flight.

From their absolute success with their programming, Checkride Prep is beginning to implement more cohorts as well. Seeing such strong feedback from just the online ground school, David wanted to expand his company even more into the aviation education sector. To do so, he's beginning a youth advocacy program.

"The whole idea behind it is really trying to offer ground school-esque content while also working to capture students' interests. As they're younger, you want to be able to diversify and have these students begin exploring different career options so that we can help them figure out what to do."

The career program David is revealing offers parents a low-cost and in-depth course for their kids, taking young and curious minds and introducing them to strong role models as well as teaching them the basics of aerospace and aeronautical science to prepare them for a potential career in the industry as pilots, technicians, astronauts, or engineers. Occurring over the course of thirty-two weeks, the program also offers flexibility for students as they tackle school and other commitments in the midst of a pandemic. The purpose of the course, David emphasizes, is to ensure that people are able to actually learn and envision themselves in the aviation world—and there shouldn't be much external pressure to do that.

Thanks to the commitment of David and Checkride Prep, thousands of prospective pilots have the opportunity to take a look into the aviation world. They're casually reminded of how they once had a dream to fly and now, with extra time on their hands, may be able to commit to that dream. Prospective pilots have an opportunity available to them to explore this world of flight at greatly reduced costs.

Both of these major initiatives are fantastic examples of what we need in the field—an opportunity to demolish the barriers to entry, ushering in fresh and curious minds from all backgrounds, and a reinforcement of that motivation by giving the next generation some role models they can look up to. By doing so, David and his crew at Checkride Prep represent the essence of advancement in the aviation world.

CHAPTER 8

SCHOLARSHIPS AND SAVING MONEY

Surprise, surprise—the cost of aviation is too high. Seems to be a recurring theme throughout this book, doesn't it? Honestly, it's probably my most overused joke:

ME, AFTER I LAND: "Ha ha, now comes the worst part of flying."

MY PASSENGER: "What's that?"

ME: "Paying for it."

Sigh. I know, I know, I shouldn't quit my day job. But nevertheless, it is true: flying is super fun and relaxing until you get that damn invoice. So how does one deal with that? I'll tell you how I did: through the use of scholarships. Come one, come all, and get ready for a crash course on aviation scholarships—the best way to pay.

One of the biggest things to look for when you're getting ready to get your license is a way to afford it. For me, this came in the form of a scholarship; for others, this might come in the form of a loan or employee discounts (companies such as Boeing or Textron Aviation provide many discounts on flight training). Not only does financial aid help you as a pilot (it's a lot easier to spend someone else's money), but pilots who receive scholarships achieve higher rates of success than those that don't.

According to a 2020 AOPA press release, the overall milestone success rate for their scholarship winners was 87 percent. This data includes students that soloed their aircraft as well as those who earned their private pilot certificate. Compare this to the AOPA statistics from a 2010 study where "approximately 60 percent of those who earn a student pilot certificate never earn a higher pilot certificate," and "many more drop out before ever receiving a student certificate… placing the overall dropout rate at an estimated 70–80 percent." In other words, success rates are about 40 percent at best for new pilots overall, versus 87 percent for those on scholarship.

Now, scholarships are the most straightforward of your financial aid options, but they too have their own problems: they're not easy to come by, and schools are not always big fans of giving them out. As a result, many are highly competitive. Larger scholarship sites where you can search specifically for an aeronautical money boost exist online. Locally (and this is where you'll have your highest chances), many museums and clubs offer them. Since these venues generally have less competitors than, say, the entire continental United States, your chances of earning a scholarship go up dramatically, and they typically cover large sums of your training or sometimes even the entirety of your license.

It should be noted that most available scholarships are for marginalized communities (first-generation, low-income, people of color, those in the LGBTQ+ community, women, etc.), or for younger pilots (high school, college, etc.). They provide much-needed opportunities that might not be possible otherwise to these communities to encourage more diversity and growth in the field of aviation. That being said, even if you do not belong to one of these groups, do your research and you will most likely find something that fits! The most important part: shoot for as many scholarships as humanly possible. You maximize your chances, and they're usually very similar in terms of application prompts. We'll also have a quick how-to on this later, but in general, if you even *think* you meet the requirements, give the application a shot. The worst they can say is no!

SEARCHING FOR APPLICATIONS

Right off the bat, you might be thinking, "Nick, there is no way that I'll ever get a scholarship. There are just too few, and I'm just not good enough for any of them."

I'll tell you that is incredibly wrong—there are many scholarships that exist in the aviation world. The true question is: how do you maximize your chances of securing one? There are a couple of rules that you'll want to remember:

1. Use your resources.
2. Apply, apply apply.

3. Apply, apply, apply (but locally this time).
4. Be prepared to not receive one.

At first glance, these seem like awful rules.

But, let's break this down further. Rule number zero: scholarships won't be known to you unless you specifically seek them out. Like a good pilot, you should use all resources available to you and look for the best scholarships for you. I'm very much against the idea of taking out a $15,000 loan, and you're probably here for that exact reason, so I'm telling you now to look for all the scholarships that you possibly can. Sites exist online for this: avscholarships.com is a great one, for example. It is important to note, however, that these scholarships (the ones that you can easily find online) are going to be pitting you up against a significant amount of competition. However, it never hurts to gather as much information as possible, and there is literally no harm in trying to apply for these major scholarships anyway. AOPA, EAA, and other aviation organizations are also fantastic places to look when browsing for a known scholarship.

Remember that scholarships are the absolute best way to pay for your flight education: you won't owe anything to anyone (other than your training), and you won't accrue any debt. This is fantastically useful: according to a 2021 article from Post University, research shows that students without a scholarship or financial aid of some form work for fifteen hours a week, sometimes more, simply to afford the cost of school, taking away from their ability to study. This increases stress and sometimes even pushes them to drop out if they struggle with balancing their job and their studies. Scholarships, of course, help fill the gap. The problem is that they can be hard to find and even harder to achieve.

So, let's say that you want to increase your chances of actually getting a scholarship (which I hope you do, unless you can afford to cough up an entire month or two of salary). Fantastic—let's do it. Most aviation scholarships aren't found online but through word of mouth at local aviation clubs.

The other day, I flew into a small airport in Astoria, Oregon. I saw a flyer for a $10,000 scholarship. It didn't exist online, and there was literally no other way to know about it unless I personally knew about the Rotary Club that funded it or if I had flown in and taken a gander at the FBO walls.

Let's do some quick math here: the city of Astoria is about ten thousand strong, and if we take the 0.2 percent of pilots in America statistic and extrapolate it, we're looking at twenty pilots in Astoria. That's it, just twenty pilots. Let's increase that number by 50 percent, just as a massive margin of error. All of a sudden, if I was gunning for a scholarship, I would have probably been in the running against about thirty others rather than the ten thousand or more that are applying for scholarships nationwide. In layman's terms, I actually have a pretty good chance.

In fact, my very own scholarship was a local one, and I not only got that private pilot scholarship but a significant college scholarship as well. The reason? I wasn't going up against such a large number of applicants. Sure, I'd like to think I'm a pretty smart guy, but once you break a certain threshold, application pools become a numbers game. And you don't need to be a mathematician to see that it's much simpler to win one in one hundred than one in ten thousand. My point being that once you do some local searching, you're more likely to get what you want. Take a risk: join some local aeronautical clubs, talk to pilots, talk to FBOs, see if your local aviation museum has anything interesting. Again, it can only help you. Who knows, maybe you'll get lucky and find a perfectly good scholarship just waiting for you to claim it.

START YOUR APPLICATIONS

On to rules one and two. You've done the hard part, searching for applications. Now you need to follow through. I applied to so many scholarships that I couldn't even keep track. Don't think about how hard it is; just do it. Set aside some time and pound out a couple of essays.

In my spare time, I help run a nonprofit called Take on College. We help first-generation, low-income students get into their dream universities by helping them directly with the college application process. Here, the scholarship process is relatively similar. Some words of advice that I always give my students:

1. Follow your values.

If there is one question that I always make my students prepare for, it's the "Why do you want this scholarship?" question. Now, the answer to that may seem obvious—you need money to fly. Duh. Well, so do the other five thousand students that are applying. The strategy is to set yourself apart by talking about your values. Ask yourself: What does the sky mean to you? What does flying mean to you? And do your best to get really emotional about it, because the more personal you are, the more interesting your essay is.

2. Make sure you keep track of your apps.

At Take on College, we use a spreadsheet to ensure students know exactly when their deadlines are, what materials they will need to submit, and who they can contact for more information. (This was born out of a tragic mistake I made—when applying to university, I misread the application deadline, forgot about it, and proceeded to turn it in very, very late. Needless to say, I did not make it into the school. So learn from my mistakes, and make yourself a spreadsheet.) If you need an example template, you can use Take on College's example. It's under our resources tab on our website: www.takeoncollege.org/resources.

Hell, once you get five to eight applications done, the rest follow pretty much the exact same format. Apply, apply, apply, and then once you think that you're done applying, apply to some more. Maximize your chances of success, because after all, this is your dream and you deserve to be able to pursue it. See, the hard part of writing is finding something to write about—the easy part is actually doing it. So get out there and apply!

HAVE A CONTINGENCY PLAN

The world of aviation can be quite turbulent. You'll quickly learn in aviation that you should hope for the best but plan for the worst. As pilots, we can't just stop flying the plane when things get tough, we have to think of a way out. Likewise, we need a plan in case scholarships don't work out.

Let's say you don't have the time to apply to a good number of scholarships or you just don't match the application requirements. AOPA (and a couple of other organizations) offers student pilot loans. The same way you can get a student loan, you can get a student pilot loan. Be careful about this one. Make sure you will be able to pay it off, and make sure that you're not getting ripped off. As always, that will require some research on your end and an evaluation of your financial ability. Loans are a great option, but I typically don't recommend them unless you know for a fact you want to go into aviation as a career—in that case, it's an investment.

The third option, as I mentioned before, is working your way through your license. Many flight schools have secretarial positions or "intern-level" positions that offer you an employee discount and limited pay. This way, you work for your flight hours. This can be quite a burden, but it is a very viable option and makes flying significantly cheaper. Consider all your options, and choose the one that you think works best for you. The end goal is the same, after all. Just make sure you have the resources (time and money) to put into this adventure so you don't have to stop halfway through (like me) and end up wasting more time than necessary.

Bottom line? Lay out the total costs in front of you, and then note your priorities and choose from there. Make sure you like how and where you are being taught, because you'll be spending close to a hundred hours with your instructor and school. In this case, cheaper is not always better. And, of course, make sure that you take a close look at your ability to pay and train. Getting the license is the easy part; planning for it is harder. Whatever the backup plan may be, make sure that you have one in place. After all, this is your dream, and where there is a will, there is a way. Just make sure you save those application essays.

THE THREE FINANCIAL BREAKDOWNS

Nowadays, you can walk into a smaller FBO and ask about flight school, and instructors are happy to talk to you about how fantastic their program is…right up until you get to the cost. From there, attitudes typically falter—a halfhearted response to the question of "will this break my bank?" The more efficient schools try to get that number out of the way painlessly. You'll get a sheet of paper that highlights the cost of the airplane per hour, the cost of the instructor per hour, and then multiplies those numbers by an average of around sixty hours. Typically, the prospective pilot will then do a double take; flying will cost about as much as a first car.

It's that precise moment that doubt begins to shadow minds. A couple grand is a big commitment, and your pilot's license will probably end up running you more than just a couple. I was fortunate enough to receive a scholarship after busting my ass on applications, and even then, I was shocked at the average costs. Again, depending on where you live, the journey to getting your pilot's license is around ten to fifteen thousand dollars. That's using an average of sixty hours toward your license, for both aircraft and instructor time, and then adding in your checkride costs, exam fees, and other flight materials (headsets, books, accessories). It's not a decision for the faint of heart by any means.

So why did I decide to bring this topic up in a book where I want to motivate people to get their license? The answer, fellow pilots, is simple: so you don't have to pay as much. So you can learn how to fly without breaking the bank (or at least, breaking the bank with less impact). There are a ton of ways to save, depending on how committed to savings and flying you are. Recently, I sat down for a few hours and worked my way through every invoice, logbook entry, and purchase I have ever made for my flight journey. From zero hours to two hundred and fifty hours—the total cost? Subtract out my scholarship ($7,000), and it cost me about $27,000—and that includes three checkrides and a new headset. The average for this, from what I was able to determine from unofficial polling, was about $50,000. So how did I do it?

1) THE WRITTEN TEST

- Ground School: $0
- Supplemental Testing Materials from the FAA: $0
- External Supplemental Testing Materials (Flight Computers, Plotters, etc.): Up to $20
- Practice Exams: $0
- The Test: about $100

TOTAL: $120

Assuming you've made up your mind to start your training, we'll begin on the ground with the most common expenses you may run into. Recall from the "Getting Started" chapter that the most expensive part of learning is the actual flying. What does that mean for you? That means the more time you can spend learning *outside* the plane, the cheaper flying will be. Start your training by signing up for *free* ground school. There are some fantastic free ones out there, like Checkride Prep. While confusing and overwhelming, ground school will set up your basic knowledge for flight. Watch videos on anything that confuses you, too. YouTube offers some great free private pilot content. Essentially, the only things you'll have to pay for are the flight computers, plotters, and sectional charts. You'll quickly learn and retain more once you can connect the dots in the air, but go ahead and start taking notes before you even step foot in the cockpit so that you can focus on flying when the time comes rather than studying.

About a third of the way through ground school, I would start my flight training. It sounds weird, but it is my opinion that training this way prevents you, the prospective pilot, from getting bored with flight before you ever even fly. Impractical knowledge through rote memorization, which sums up ground school to a tee, is typically the bigger worry for pilots in training. You'll likely feel like you are drinking from a fire hose by this point in the class as well, so it's a great time for you to actually apply that knowledge in the cockpit. That way, you'll understand what exactly you're doing and will be able to fill in some gaps in your knowledge that ground school just doesn't cover that well.

Tempting as it may be to just learn by flying, don't. This is something I did when I pursued my license, and it ended up biting me in the ass once my checkride rolled around. I had to delay my ride by an entire month solely because I couldn't schedule my written exam in time. Instead, roll with the punches: on the days that you don't fly, study. Get through those ground lessons, and then use a free online practice test (Sporty's Study Buddy or the PSI testing service) to evaluate yourself. You'll begin noticing patterns in the questions that you're asked, and you'll quickly begin to piece together the answers to those questions. Don't spend your time wondering why a question is wrong, just search it up and check out the dozens of explanations online. If it doesn't make sense, ask your CFI—they are there to help you. A good rule of thumb that most instructors use is this: once you get three to five 90 percent or higher practice exam scores in a row, you're ready to sign up for and take the written test.

Navigate online to the PSI testing center website, and search for your closest PSI testing site. You could take the test at your local flight school, too, but keep in mind that this will cost you an additional sixty dollars in testing fees (charged by PSI). Save yourself the money, and just get it done at a PSI facility.

Get that written exam out of the way as soon as humanly possible, so that you can focus on pure flying. It'll be a lot more fun, and you'll find that you retain a lot of the knowledge you learned, seeing that you'll apply a significant portion of it while training.

2) FLIGHT COSTS
- Aircraft Rental: 60 hours at $125 an hour: $7,500
- Instructor for Flight: 60 hours at $60 an hour: $3,600
- Instructor for Ground Lessons and Briefings: 20 hours at $60 an hour: $1,200
- External Costs (Headsets, Medical Exam, Accessories): $1,000

TOTAL: Too Much ($13,300)

Ouch. That hurt to type, and it still hurts to read. No one wants to spend this much on flight training, so here's a quick couple of paragraphs on saving that dough.

I'll make this quick: there's not much you can do to save money on your medical exam or accessories, so go ahead and just get those out of the way. Buy once, cry once for these items. Headsets are a bit different—depending on your aviation goals I would get a nice one. If you see yourself flying for awhile, go ahead and bite the bullet on some nice Bose or Lightspeed sets, otherwise keep it simple and durable. Crazed-pilot and a couple of other stores have sweet deals on headsets that are decent and won't make you gasp at the price tag.

First off, like I mentioned before, get out of the cockpit. Flight costs are the most expensive part of training, so do yourself a favor and don't fly as much.

But Nick, you may be asking, don't I want to fly more to become a better pilot?

Yes. Absolutely, yes. But you have to be smart about it—chair fly your lessons, and review them on the ground so you aren't lost in the air.

Ask your instructor for a lesson plan beforehand. What maneuvers are you doing that day? What points are you supposed to demonstrate? Once you have this information, crack open that book, or, if you are like me and want to save time, open up that YouTube app and search for your specific lesson. I've learned a lot from watching these online videos, and though nothing beats the real thing, these sure can help. Plop yourself down in your chair, and verbally and physically reenact your flight—before each flight. This trains your mind so that you aren't completely lost and trains your muscles so that they don't have to play catchup with your mind five thousand feet in the air. I've seen students get through training in minimal hours by doing this, saving themselves about two thousand dollars in the process.

The second part to saving money on flight training is time. Start your training in spring or summer. You'll get the most out of sunny days and nice weather, and you'll have a little more free time to fly. Sorry to you busy folks out there, but if you aren't fitting in three lessons a week, you're probably spending more than necessary. Why? Because you aren't using the knowledge that you're learning on a consistent basis. Flying an airplane is an intensive process, and if you aren't using that skill, you're losing it. Consistency and frequency, apart from being prepared, are the best and easiest ways to save money, however ironic it may seem.

Don't get me wrong, you'll probably have days when getting into that cockpit is the last thing that you want to do. There will be spans where you plateau and it feels like you're just burning money by flying. But without that consistency, you're losing a very volatile skill—it's not exactly riding a bike. If you don't do it, you won't remember it. Power through these days, vary your training lessons, do what you need to do, but get yourself into the air and flying. Again, don't be like me: I kicked off my training in fall, and had to essentially restart once the summer rolled around—not good for me or my wallet.

Additionally, and this goes without saying, use simulators as much as you can. From the simple Microsoft Flight Simulators to the real Advanced Training Devices that your flight school has, these machines will be much cheaper than your real airplanes. Get that sim time in; it's easier than chair fly and trains you well for actual flight. The thought process here is simple: why spend money on the real thing when the fake one works almost as well?

3) THE CHECKRIDE
- The Exam: $550–$850
- The Airplane: 1.5 hours at $125 an hour: $188

TOTAL: Up to $1000

How do you save money on a checkride? Don't.

Wait, what? Yes—your checkride is your way to show once and for all that you are a fully competent, proficient, and safe pilot. If you're trying to rush through your checkride and save $50 on airplane time, you're setting yourself up for failure. I'm all about saving money, folks, but you may want to bite the bullet on this one.

There is a way, however, to make sure that you save a couple hundred dollars beforehand, and that is to be prepared. Don't get "unsat," and make sure you know your stuff down pat. Do you really want to pay another four hundred dollars just to retake the exam due to a silly error? No. You don't. You can shop around for good DPEs and choose the one that charges you the least, but make sure you know what you're doing, otherwise all that work is for nothing. Good luck and blue skies, pilot.

Other ways to save money include:

1. Finding a compatible instructor. Shop around and get yourself someone you can relate to who understands your goals and motivations. A good instructor is worth dozens of flight hours, as they help mold not only you and your skills as a pilot but your confidence and mentality in the flight training process.
2. Find a strong pilot community. Get online and join some flying groups. Pilots are well-connected and more than willing to help. Need some help preparing for a training lesson? Ask the group. Need a mock oral exam? Ask the group. Generally, ask and you will receive is a rule that runs pretty well in these groups—just remember to give back to the community.

All in all, flying is expensive. Make it less so by staying determined to be successful. Take it flight by flight, and you'll find that your dreams are very much within your reach.

ACTION CHECKLIST FOR SAVING MONEY:

☑ Research, research, research. Find those scholarships.

☑ Apply, apply, apply. The more you apply, the higher your chances of winning something.

☑ Shop around. See what you could save on, and see what you should splurge on. It'll save you money if you do this before hopping into the cockpit.

☑ Break down your flight costs. It's important to identify what costs you money and to have a good estimate on spending.

☑ Make Friends in the Aviation Community

☑ Friends are great. They let you practice things (for free!) like Mock Orals and sometimes even flights!

☑ Friends are also your number one resource for finding hidden gems, like local scholarships!

CHAPTER 9

HOW TO GET YOUR LICENSE: PREFLIGHT CHECKLIST

———

So you're considering it. You've looked up at the sky enough, and you're finally beginning to wonder—what would it be like to see the world from above? You think about it some more, enjoying the imagery, and that is when reality hits. How much would it all cost? How long will it all take? Where would you even start?

Many potential aviators are stopped by the overwhelming task of getting their pilot's license—how to do it, where to learn from, and how much you'll pay for it. Often, a younger person won't have the time to process all this and thus won't make the jump into aviation. So for those of you reading this book and thinking about getting your license, I won't let that stop you: this story is all about how you can get your license—and how to do it affordably.

I remember when I first got started. The path was clear as mud. I was presented with the costs upfront and had no real idea of how the process worked other than knowing I would fly with an instructor until I was proficient enough to pass the final test. Only when I began the training and dug into the process did I truly begin to understand how things worked. It actually wasn't until after I had gotten my license that I was able to take a step back and truly analyze how I could've saved money and time.

One of the benefits of aviation is that there are so many great paths to get from point A to point B. That flexibility, though, also happens to be one of its downfalls. With so many paths, how do you know what is best for you? Throughout this book, I present you with some viable options to highlight some of the more efficient paths I have seen. So strap in, because here is a crash course on the logistics behind getting your license.

STEP 0: ACKNOWLEDGE THE MONSTROUS TASK AHEAD OF YOU

The first step is to acknowledge the monstrous task ahead of you. It's not easy, and you should accept that. Don't let it stop you, though. Once that's all done and you've seen the mountain to be moved, it's time for you to break it up into achievable tasks. The most important step is to sign up for a discovery flight. These are relatively inexpensive flights that will allow you to not only get a cheap hour of flight, but also help you decide whether this is something that you'll have fun doing. My first discovery flight was a great way for me to see how fun flying could be and how beautiful the world looked from above.

You should also know ahead of time how much cash you'll need to burn to achieve your goals. Some pilots I've talked to refuse to keep track of the money they spend on aviation, since it's their guilty pleasure. But, if you're like me and hate to waste money, I highly recommend you keep track of your expenses to make sure you are on track. Plan ahead, and you'll be able to achieve your flying dreams and save a couple thousand dollars, as well as hours of your time.

STEP 1: LEARN HOW TO LEARN

Part 61 or Part 141? If you've never stepped foot in the aviation world before, these words may not sound like anything to you. But they'll be the heart of how you conduct your training, so you should get a good definition at the start.

Part 61 and Part 141 are the shorthand names of the two different ways to learn to fly. Pilots operate with rules from the Federal Aviation Regulations, also known as the FARs (specifically, section 14 of the Code of Federal Regulations). These FARs have various parts that you'll pick up as you train, but the first ones you should get familiar with are Part 61 (dealing with how pilots are able to get their licenses) and Part 141 (dealing with aviation academies and flight schools with set lesson plans).

To compare the two, I turned to my friend Sameer Romani, a freshly minted commercial pilot out of the Part 141 flight program at the University of North Dakota (UND).

"Having had experience with both, I can confidently say I prefer the 141 environment over 61 any day, but it's not without its flaws. Firstly, Part 141 flight training introduces the student to a more structured flight process, complete with stage checks to pass from one block to the next and an orderly flow of lessons to follow before they are signed off for their checkride. It gives a clear understanding of flight training progression and has been advantageous for my personal development as a pilot."

Sameer makes a crucial point: one of the biggest benefits of Part 141 training is knowing exactly where you are during the training process and when you as a student can reasonably expect to be finished with the specific license you are working on. For those of you that find yourselves constantly asking, "How much do I have left?" Part 141 may be the program for you. This is essentially plane school—you are quite literally in a heavily regimented class. Schedule your flights at these times; this is the lesson plan for the day; your stage check will be during this week. What's more, the school offers the discipline and accountability that so many new pilots may lack, as well as clarity to a very complex program.

Additionally, Part 141 exchanges flexibility for speed. These schools are generally paid for up front so that students can forget about the cost and just grind out flight hours and instruction. Because of their rigid and focused structure, Part 141 pilots often have lower flight time requirements: thirty-five hours minimum to receive your Private Pilot License rather than forty, for example. I would highly recommend Part 141 if you have the money up front and know that you are ready to jump into the world of aviation. The fast-paced and structured learning style isn't for everyone, but the great thing about Part 141 is that it enforces flight lessons, which give many pilots the extra push they need to finish their training. Due to their structure, these programs are also more likely to accept scholarships, grants, and any other waivers or discounts (more on that later).

That being said, those of you who are "weekend pilots"—the ones juggling a few jobs and school, the ones who don't have a ton of time—will want to go through your training under Part 61. That is where Sameer notes that Part 61 does have a few advantages.

"The biggest advantage Part 61 has over 141 is the freedom of flexibility. As an illustration, let's say the student doesn't pass their stage check to move into the next block. In Part 61, lessons in the following block can still be conducted whereas in Part 141, time needs to be spent reviewing deficiencies before the student can reattempt the stage and move forward."

Essentially, a Part 141 school allots a specific amount of training for students to perform each task. Once that training is up, students are expected to progress to their stage check—which, if failed, prevents you from moving forward in your training until your deficient maneuvers or skills are properly addressed. Meanwhile, a Part 61 student could continue with their training while also practicing the deficient maneuver.

Part 61 is how I did my training; higher flexibility was (and still is) better for me. While I still strongly recommend flying at least twice a week, Part 61 allows more flexibility in what you work on for each flight. This means that students are able to slow down and take the time to work on things that they don't feel confident in—at the expense of cost and time, of course. However, done correctly, this method can also be a great way to save money. Because there is no standardized curriculum, you only need to pay for what you need and not much else (and flight club/instructor rates are typically much cheaper than at a Part 141 school). As long as you fly often and study hard, there is a good chance you can finish your training just as quickly as a Part 141 student and save yourself a ton of money!

Pick the solution that best fits your schedule and budget. No matter which method you choose, both will earn you the same qualifications at the end of the day. Other than for your checkride, no one is going to be asking you whether you did your training under Part 61 or Part 141.

STEP 2: CONSIDER THE COSTS

Once you've decided what's best for you, it's time to window-shop. For those of you in cities with many small airports, this will require much more work, as flight training prices often vary a good amount even between flight schools in the "same" area. The good thing is you have more options. On the flip side, this means you will have to do more homework. Do your due diligence and calculate not only estimated costs (using Excel), but also factor in your commute from your house or work to the airport.

For example, I was able to find a fantastic flight club in the Seattle area with extraordinarily affordable rates located about an hour away from me. Alternatively, I could go to my local airport and fly out of there for a much larger bite out of my wallet. However, factor in the commute, and the far-away flight club actually turned out to be more expensive. Make sure you account for all your variables when you look around. In addition to costs, factors such as flexibility (cancellation fees, instructor changes), availability (when are you able to rent a plane?), and—simply put—the *vibe* of the school are important to consider.

Another unique idea: getting a Sport Pilot License (SPL). Let's say you just want to fly and sometimes bring up a friend with you every now and then: a Sport Pilot License may be the move for you. Specifically created to offer more affordable ways to enter the aviation world, the SPL gives you *most* of the same privileges as a Private Pilot, but you are now restricted to two-seat aircraft only (along with a plethora of other restrictions, some of which can be lifted with additional training—and are all available via Google search).

According to a 2020 article written by Dan Pimentel for *Flying* Magazine, "The average cost for a Sport Pilot License can be as low as $4,400." This is due in part to the relaxed training requirements: to qualify for the SPL, you only need twenty total hours instead of the forty mandated for your PPL. "Those [savings] reflect a course of training to the minimum FAA-mandated flight-hour requirements." Pimentel also spoke with Dan Johnson, who added that while the planes that sport pilots are eligible to fly are smaller, lighter, and often slower than most private aircraft, this does not mean that they are in any way low-performance or antiquated. In fact, Light Sport Aircraft (LSA) often boast incredible digital technology in the cockpit along with modern Rotax engines that "produce the same amounts of power as older legacy engines, thus burning far less fuel per hour." Additionally, proposed rule changes may expand the types of aircraft that can be piloted with a Sport Pilot License, tacking on popular aircraft such as the Cessna 172 (the workhorse of general aviation today). If your end goal is to have some fun in the sky with just you and a buddy, the SPL might be your best bet.

Whichever your end goal, PPL or SPL, make sure you plan ahead and consider all the costs that could be involved.

STEP 3: BEFORE YOU TAKE OFF

Almost done! You're almost there, and all it took was a couple of hours of research and two major decisions. Hang in there; you'll get to the fun part soon. This step is where you schedule your ground work, your medical appointments, and your insurance and finalize your timeline so that you can focus on the flying and not on the dreary paperwork.

Flight training is typically set up in two parts: the ground school and the physical application. Ground school is exactly what it sounds like: flying school on the ground. This is where you'll learn the basic laws and regulations of flight that you'll need to know for your written exam and your practical checkride. Ground school is best described as "drinking from a fire hose," and for good reason: you'll be bombarded with new, confusing information such as numbers that are important to flight but seem to be pulled out of thin air; various regulations that affect how, when, and where you can fly; and a ton of other things.

As a result, it's best to combine the ground school with your lessons: you'll get the confusing information first then apply it in real life as you fly! It makes it at least a little bit less overwhelming (and a lot less boring). As a result, I'd schedule the ground school to coincide with your first few lessons. This way, you can get it out of the way and take the written exam so you don't have to worry about it later in your training and so you retain the information by actually applying it in flight.

Luckily, there are tons of ground school resources out there. You might recall the *free* online ground schools. Checkride Prep Aviation Academy and Sling Aviation Academy offer some great online ground schools that are recorded and free. Attend all the classes and pass the final practice exam, and they even offer you the chance to receive your endorsement. I highly recommend this path for those of you on a budget and those of you that are just looking into flight. Once you've taken the ground lessons, go ahead and use Sporty's Study Buddy (also free—do you see a pattern?) which gives you the same types of questions that you'll see on the official Federal Aviation Administration (FAA) Written Exam, and they're almost verbatim.

Next up is your medical exam, and this is where a problem exists for many pilots. While it isn't hard to schedule an appointment to take your medical exam, the FAA is cautious about the medications you take and any physical barriers that you might encounter in flight. Things like color blindness, usage of antidepressants, and diabetes may automatically put you at risk of not getting your medical certificate. While I am not a certified aeronautical medical examiner, I would make sure that you know how these things affect your ability to secure your medical clearance.

While all these things are sorted out, you'll be able to sit down with your flight instructor and secure your student pilot certificate. This Student License, in addition to a government-issued ID and your newly-minted medical certificate, allows you to fly an aircraft by yourself (with the authorization and endorsement of a CFI). You are eligible for this license if you are sixteen years old and can read, speak, and understand English. Keep in mind that you do not need a Student License to take flying lessons (although it is much easier to get it out of the way before you start).

As a reminder, you do not need anything other than a desire to get started with flying to receive this license: you don't have to be signed up with a ground school or even have your medical ready. Officially, you fill out an online form (FAA Form 8710-1) via the online Integrated Airman Certification and Rating Application (IACRA) and submit it to a Flight Standards Certification Office (free) or your CFI (could charge you money). That may sound like a lot, but in reality, it is a quick Google search for "IACRA" followed by a thirty-second sign-up and a five-minute form. Not too bad for being allowed to fly a plane all by yourself!

Lastly, you might want to get some renter's insurance depending on your school or flight club policy. Some schools offer a very comprehensive package in terms of insurance, and you won't have to worry about it. Others may have bare-bones plans that require you to have your own insurance. Make sure you read through the terms and conditions and understand the answers to any questions that you may have. Popular insurance brokers are AOPA and USAA, though there are definitely more that may charge you less. Make sure you shop around and get the best rates that you can. If you're already blowing your bank account on flying, why not try to minimize the damage?

Alright! Let's say you've done all those things. Enough boring stuff. Let's go fly!

ACTION CHECKLIST FOR GETTING YOUR LICENSE:

☑ Acknowledge the huge step you just took: you're going to become a pilot!

☑ Create a pros and cons list of how you would like your training to go: Part 61 or Part 141? Highlight the decision you make and commit.

☑ Research your options. Get a spreadsheet together on the flight schools and clubs within your community, and see how much each one costs.

☑ Hint: Make sure you take your time! Plan ahead, and you will save money!

☑ Choose the school that works best for you!

☑ Get ready to fill out some paperwork:

☑ Get your medical certificate. You need this before you can fly!

☑ Get your insurance sorted out. Do some win-dow-shopping for the best deals!

☑ Sign up for ground school. It's important you get familiar with the laws of the sky!

☑ Talk to your CFI and fill out your IACRA. They will help you with this.

☑ Schedule your first discovery flight!

CHAPTER 10

HOW TO GET YOUR LICENSE: TAKING TO THE SKIES

"Flying isn't dangerous. Crashing is what's dangerous." Welcome back! Hopefully, you've gotten that last checklist completed, because here comes the fun: the flying. Don't go thinking that you're home free just yet, though!

STEP 4: GO FLY

Once you find your school, go ahead and get started by scheduling your first lesson. While the costs of flight are astonishing, many schools offer "block time." These are multi-hour blocks that you pay for up front at a significantly discounted price. They require an initial payment typically in the thousands, but you'll end up saving a couple hundred dollars since the schools then discount your hourly rates. I recommend going with this option if you have the ability to do so, as it is the most cost effective: at a *minimum*, you'll need forty hours of flying, so simply purchasing that time now enables you to fly at a discount rather than paying as you go.

I couldn't afford block time when I began training, so I had to go with the pay-as-you-fly option. Luckily, there is a way to save yourself money with this option as well, and that is to come prepared for your lesson. In our age of information, there are so many great and free training resources available online that you can pretty much chair fly every lesson so that it's not all new to you in the air—saving you even more hundreds of dollars.

Chair flying—think of this as pretend flying by using your imagination—is a great way to develop muscle memory and work through any potential issues you may not catch when just reading about what to do. Visualize your controls in front of you and flow through your checklists as if you were really flying the airplane. It sounds silly, but think about it: chair flying costs you nothing, and real flying costs you hundreds of dollars an hour—and it's not like anyone is going to be judging you when you're alone in your room. Chair flying allows you to memorize checklists and get some basic muscle memory in, and best of all, you get to connect with your childhood imagination. What fun!

Another thing I highly recommend is getting up in the air at least twice a week. Aviation, as mentioned before, is very much a "use it or lose it" skill, and not being able to fly often will mean that you are, effectively, losing it. It's super important to find a good schedule for you not only as a human but as a pilot, so that the things you learn come together a lot faster and more cohesively. I've never seen a good student pilot that flew only every other week, and that includes myself. When the weather was bad in Seattle, it meant that I was stuck on the ground. By the time the weather had cleared up, I was effectively starting over, which was not too much fun after putting in four grand, not to mention the frustration of not being able to nail a maneuver that I had spent countless hours on before. If nothing else, the best way to save money is by learning quickly, and you can ensure that by training often.

Take it from my flight instructor, D'artagnan Heath: "I fully recommend that you fly as often as possible. There is no substitute for experience. I would often see students come in thinking they can fly once a week—be careful with that. I would say any less than two times a week and you don't retain enough to progress."

As you fly, you'll pick up tips and tricks that come with experience. The engine will have a "correct" sound, the fast communications on the radio become second nature, and the landings get smoother and less nerve-racking. It's important to note, however, that flying is not easy. I've mentioned it before, and I'll mention it again—flying is a learned skill. Just like driving a car, you have to study and spend time practicing before it all comes together. The difference with airplanes, though, is that you have to throw in an entirely new dimension which complicates things quite a bit. Don't get discouraged when you get stuck!

Think about it: you're doing something that is completely unnatural to you. You're leaving the nice, safe ground and climbing in an airplane and *flying*. Of course it'll be hard; of course it'll take some time. You're doing what your ancestors always dreamed of doing, and you're learning it as you go. Just remember: as you fly, you're making a place for yourself in the sky. It won't always be easy, but it'll always be worth it.

STEP 5: THE FIRST SOLO
(AND ALL THE SOLOS AFTER THAT)

They say you never forget your first. My first solo was July 18th, 2018. I was flying a Cessna 150, N45517. I took off from Bremerton Airport, KPWT, did three laps in the pattern, and then landed. Other than the fact that some traffic decided to over-fly the runway in the opposite direction as I turned for final (which scared the shit out of me), there was nothing unusual. And yet, it was one of the most important flights of my life.

The importance of the solo is never lost on the student. Take it from Addie, my friend who is days away from taking her private pilot checkride. "When I first took off solo, I screamed— not out of fear, but out of excitement. It was the first time I was in the airplane alone, and it felt amazing." Addie's experience with her first solo gave her something essential in her development as a proficient pilot: "All of the solo flying I did taught me that I can absolutely make it work—I have the critical thinking skills and [Aeronautical Decision Management] to make sure that I won't die. My confidence absolutely skyrocketed—it was the notion that I was flying, and that I was able to do it without anyone next to me."

Here, you've proven that you're ready to take an airplane up into the sky all by yourself, and less than one percent of the world can say the same. It's a huge milestone, and you should be proud. As my CFI, Joseph Merlino, points out: "I'd say it's the flying equivalent of hitting your first home run in baseball. It's the most freeing experience I think you can have in a piece of machinery. You're truly flying for the first time, because everything you do up there is absolutely on you." I had the pleasure of being the very first student pilot that Joseph was able to send solo, also an incredible feeling for the instructor who has been teaching you since that very first day.

Of course, as with any first time, there can be nerves. You no longer have someone who can save you; you're the official pilot in command. That means that your instructor has seen you fly so well and has seen you so prepared to take on emergencies that they're ready to let you go out into the flying world all alone. In classic *National Geographic* style, let's do a step-by-step narration of what your first solo flight will look like—and try to imagine David Attenborough's voice on top of this.

As the young pilot becomes smarter and smarter, the experienced CFI begins to prepare him for his first flight alone. It's a beautiful sight to see as they cautiously release the controls, placing not only the student's life in the hands of a new pilot, but their own. As the student gently nudges the aircraft to a smooth landing, the CFI can often be seen beaming with pride.

Cue the dramatic music here.

Confident that the student is ready to go off on his own, the CFI nods. The pair exchange a few excited words, and the student is ready to go fly without the help of the instructor. He excitedly begins his taxi to the runway, as the proud CFI looks on from the ramp.

Music swells here.

The first solo for a young pilot is nothing short of spectacular. It's the first time they will be taking to the skies all by themselves. Despite knowing the student is ready, the CFI stands by, ready to spring into action in case of any emergencies. The student slowly brings the airplane into the air. They've done it! Watch as they soar in the pattern, doing one lap after another. Of course, their landing might not be the best—ouch—but the important part is that they're ready to fly, and fly they do. Satisfied by the student's performance, the CFI gives a subtle smile. This young pilot is not just another student any more.

Fade out music and scene transition.

Now, back to our regularly scheduled programming.

The thing that no one tells you when you solo is how confidence-boosting it is. That airplane that you thought may have been a bit slow and sluggish suddenly seems to sprout rocket engines. Without the weight of your instructor, you feel like you're absolutely zooming through the skies—and when you start to do everything correctly and smoothly, it all comes together.

I will tell you right now, that confidence high stuck with me for days. The importance of this flight, other than it being your first one alone, is that it proves to you that you are, without a doubt, capable of being a real pilot. That is a feat in itself and the real reason we have solos worked into our training. As you progress farther and farther, you'll learn more and more difficult things, but for now, you have the confidence of someone who has survived a flight all by themselves—a priceless gift.

STEP 6: THE (REAL) TEST PART 1

Let's fast forward a bit—you've learned a lot from your instructor, you've been perfecting your maneuvers, and you're on the cusp of wrapping up. Oh man, if you were nervous for your written exam, just wait until your checkride date. Coming from someone who had to come in for their checkride twice (discontinuance due to weather), the butterflies are serious.

The checkride is aptly named: it's a ride-along flight for your FAA certified, designated pilot examiner (DPE) to confirm whether you are capable of handling an airplane competently and proficiently. Oh, and if you fail to prove proficiency, it goes on your permanent flight record. In other words, it's the real deal. These don't come cheap either. You can expect checkrides to run between four hundred and one thousand dollars (with a reexamination fee of probably half what you paid initially). Yikes! I know. No pressure, right? To ensure you pass the first time around, let's break it down.

As mentioned earlier, there are two parts to your official checkride: the oral portion and the flight portion. Many pilots, including myself, find themselves worrying more about the oral. This is a lengthy exam in which you'll be asked to explain your way through some very practical situations; there are no multiple-choice answers. Questions like "What would you do in this situation?" and "What is the best way to handle this emergency?" are to be expected. With the way orals are structured, it's hard to stay relaxed, but do your best. This is simply a culmination of all the flying knowledge you've picked up from day zero to now. No worries! Your oral exam is a lot like an interview; you definitely know the material, but can you perform well under pressure?

In a 2020 interview, when asked what he was most comfortable with going in for the oral portion, Nicholas Shelton, a BoldMethod team member said, "I was scared that I wouldn't be able to answer the questions the DPE gave me—not for a lack of knowledge, but rather from my inability to articulate the information to my examiner." To combat that, Shelton focused a lot of his preparation time on answering commonly asked questions so that he would be prepared to clearly and effectively answer any questions when the time came. "By rehearsing these questions ahead of time," Shelton said, "I was a lot less nervous on checkride day."

Shelton was smart in the way that he answered his questions. "I tried to answer everything concisely and not expand on my answers beyond what was asked." This part is truly important: a common reason that students fail their checkride is their over-explanations. DPEs are more than happy to listen to you talk and won't be stopping you if you say something wrong. In fact, they might even ask more questions about it to see just how deep you'll dig. Keep your answers short and sweet. If you know something, state the answer. If you don't, try and find it in the exam books you've brought along, and don't waste time admitting you don't know if the answer isn't plainly obvious. It's silly to have to pay for a reexamination because you dug yourself into a hole of misinformation.

Toward the end of the interview, Shelton was asked the most unexpected question he was given. "My examiner asked me a question about scuba diving. I distinctly remember thinking, 'This is it, I have failed my exam because of some obscure scuba diving regulation,' but it wasn't." Why? Shelton knew where to look up such regulations. The oral portion is open note. You can access any and all FAA aviation resources and even some of your own. Of course, this doesn't give you free reign to simply Google every answer, but if you find one or two that trip you up, keep calm and look through your documents.

"It's important to remember that you can't know everything, and a pilot who thinks they do is more dangerous than a pilot who is willing to admit they don't have an answer. At this point, the checkride seemed less like an exam and more like a discussion with someone who was just as interested in aviation as I was."

While the oral exam is a nerve-racking experience, it certainly doesn't have to be. Think about it: you've been flying and studying since your first day in the air, and so you know much, much more than you might think you do. You haven't hurt yourself or others in the air either (hopefully), so you evidently know enough to keep yourself alive and well. That being said, it's definitely a good idea to get some practice in. Online, you'll find some free oral guides. For those of you that just want to splurge on an official prep book, ASA offers a great guide book (I say splurge, but it's only fifteen dollars. You can probably find some cheaper, honestly.) that covers every private pilot topic under the sun.

Once you have the online guide or the prep book, simply drill these questions as often as possible. You'll find that you know a surprising amount of them—and those that you don't, you can mark and study up on. You should have a pretty general idea of how these questions go, so I won't recap them here. Just remember that you don't need to know every single thing, you just need to be able to practically apply your knowledge of flight rules and regulations, as well as your sense of self-preservation and safety. Questions like "What are your personal flight weather minimums?" should be answered in such a fashion, and keep in mind that just because something is legal, doesn't mean it's smart.

The oral exam will also come a lot smoother if you have a general idea of what to expect: try and get a "gouge" on your DPE (a gouge is a write-up by another pilot on their specific DPE, and it goes over what the DPE tends to focus on and what areas you will want to have down). These gouges are really useful to have: it's kind of like having the test before the actual test day. If you know beforehand what you should be focusing on, then you don't have an excuse to not prepare!

So, to recap: your oral exam is probably the most nerve-racking part of the checkride. You have to know and understand a seemingly mountainous pile of information. Not only that, you have to verbally explain what you know to a complete stranger—not what I would call fun in any circumstance. However, treat it like any other exam, get a good amount of practice in, know what to expect, and you'll be ready to kill it and move on to the easy part: flying.

STEP 7: THE (REAL) TEST PART 2

Woohoo! You just explained everything that you know about aviation for probably an hour or more, and you're feeling euphoric that you passed. Now it's time for your flight portion. This is now your opportunity to demonstrate just what an amazing pilot you are and also a place where many students get "unsat" (where they receive a grade of "unsatisfactory," or, in layman's terms, fail).

According to the FAA, about 24 percent of students do not pass their checkride the first time around (AvWeb, 2017). This may result from various factors: maybe they were too nervous, maybe they had a brain fart, maybe they just were not ready. Either way, they do not pass go and do not collect two hundred dollars. Luckily, this isn't the end of the world—many companies don't mind one or two failed checkrides—so long as you are honest about what you did wrong and are clear about what you learned from the experience. A failed checkride, while unfortunate, will not hurt your long-term chances. That being said, we don't want to fail, so let's jump into it.

When you first schedule your checkride, you should receive a couple requests for paperwork and a request for a flight plan.

The flight plan that you'll be doing is based on your own decision. The DPE typically gives you a cross-country location and a couple of stipulations (maybe they have a small bladder and must land every two hours, or maybe they have to check in on their pet canary often and require an internet connection) and then asks for you to plan a safe and successful flight out to that location. You'll then choose where you want your waypoints to be, where you might want to land and why, and all the rest of the important things you'll need to know to successfully and safely fly an aircraft. I forgot to mention earlier, but this flight plan will also be the basis of at least a few of the questions in your oral exam, so make sure you can explain just about every decision you've made: takeoff calculations, weight and balance calculations, estimated time en route. Those are all important to know, especially for this portion.

In all, depending on how you plan your flight, the process is not one that you want to procrastinate—start early and make sure you are making the right decisions.

Once you and your DPE have briefed the flight, it's time for you to take to the skies and show them what you've got. This next part is crucial: use your checklists. I cannot emphasize this enough. Pilots have checklists for a reason, and that reason is so that they don't forget anything while in the stressful environment of an aircraft. Checklists help you stay ahead of the airplane, and they literally tell you everything that you may have to do. In fact, they're so useful that a lot of us tend to forget to use them—maybe we think they make flight too easy or something. At any rate, make sure that you are in the habit of using your checklists. Verbally call out every single item. Make a show of it, too: your checklists will be your best friend for this checkride. Why? Your DPE will be looking to make sure you have good flying habits, and reading your checklists is perhaps the easiest way to tell if you're being a good pilot.

The DPEs aren't just being annoying, or strict, either. A groundbreaking 1990 Human Factors study from NASA researcher Asaf Dagani noted the importance of the checklist, particularly during takeoff, approach, and landing.

"Although these segments comprise only 27 percent of average flight duration, they account for 76.3 percent of hull-loss accidents," he wrote. In the article, Dagani studied why the checklist was so important and why, even in the larger aircrafts that operate today, the checklist is sometimes inadvertently skipped. Despite its importance, many pilots respond to checklist items as complete even if they are not, simply because "it was what they expected to see." In the case of Spanair flight 5022, that was exactly what happened: the crew of the flight forgot to set the flaps correctly during the after-start checklist, ran through two additional checklists in preparation for takeoff, and did not notice the flaps were up, because they expected them to be. The aircraft crashed, killing 154 of the 172 on board.

The usage of checklists is not essential only to aviation: Atul Gawande, an author and a surgeon, created a simple surgical team communications checklist for use in operating rooms. "We implemented it in eight hospitals. The average reduction in complications was 36 percent," he told the *Harvard Business Review* in 2010. "We cut deaths by almost half, all those results being highly statistically significant."

Despite all the evidence backing the importance of proper checklist usage, many pilots develop bad habits as they fly and seem to just "remember how to do things." Don't forget, however, that flying has never been a forgiving activity, and the incorporation of checklists ensures that you don't miss anything essential in the first place.

Think about it: you don't ever have to get that sinking feeling that you're missing anything anymore because your checklists will tell you. It might be simple for you to memorize what to do in a small Cessna, but your DPE will want to see that you still err on the side of caution like a good and safe pilot and use your damn checklist. And I will let you in on a secret. If you do end up forgetting something that you can (and should) simply "look up," that surely won't bode well for you and your goals of getting that license you paid so much for. Long story short: use your checklists, please.

Whew, that was a lot. Now that you won't ever forget to use a checklist again, let's see what else we need to do. You'll complete your preflight checklist, then hop in with your DPE, and start up the aircraft. From there, it's just like any other flight—except that you're in charge, no one will help you, and your DPE will act like a judgmental ghost. The flight will differ from examiner to examiner, but each one will contain the exact same material you must cover in order to receive your license.

These standards are known as the Airmen Certification Standards (ACS) and are released and updated annually by the FAA for public use. The creation of the ACS was no accident either: many years ago, the FAA created the Pilot Testing Standards, or PTS, to objectively evaluate pilot proficiency and risk management. Over the course of its existence, the PTS became bloated, if you will. It was a bit too broad in defining what was acceptable for pilot checkrides, and many complained that questions on the PTS were "overly broad, overly complex, trivial, outdated, and sometimes irrelevant" (FAA ACS FAQs 2020). Kind words, as you can see. At any rate, it was clear that DPEs needed a way to evaluate pilots objectively, and CFIs needed a clear expectation of what to teach. As a result, the ACS was born and, with it, a much clearer picture of what you need to show in order to receive your license.

The ACS tells you what you need to be able to accomplish and exactly how accurately or precisely you must accomplish it. For example, when performing a maneuver such as a steep turn, pilots must be able to demonstrate that they can maintain a 45-degree bank for a full 360-degree turn, without losing or gaining more than one hundred feet of altitude and without deviating from course by more than 10 degrees. As you can see, there is not much room for misinterpretation. These are numbers you should memorize so you know that you are within the ACS margins of error when you're practicing. Keep in mind that under the pressure of a real checkride your flying will get worse, so I took each ACS limit and halved it and refused to schedule a checkride until I knew for sure that I could hit those stricter targets every time. Sure, it may be a little nitpicky, but this allowed me to have a huge margin of error during my exam. I was used to only having fifty feet of error, but now I had one hundred—which really helped with my nerves when I was flying the real thing. By doing so, I also ensured that I could pass 100 percent of the maneuvers and wouldn't get "unsat" on my checkride.

A couple of other tips in preparation for your checkride: make sure you fly the airplane first and foremost. You are the pilot in command, and so you can treat the flight as such—in fact, acting like pilot in command is essential to passing a checkride. If you aren't comfortable doing something that isn't required, just say so and stand by your decision. After all, the DPE is just a judgmental "ghost;" they're just there to observe, not complain.

The second thing is to make sure you know what you're doing. You may have practiced the maneuvers well, but have you practiced with distractions? Have you made sure that you can still fly the aircraft first and foremost even when tasks begin to pile up? Remember that it is important to first aviate, then navigate, and finally, communicate. Don't forget that. Aviate, Navigate, Communicate. This catchy phrase serves us pilots as an important reminder to fly the airplane first in stressful situations, then get to where you need to go, and finally talk to others about your plans. While communication is key in the sky, if you're in the middle of a task and the DPE is rapidly firing questions at you, don't be afraid to take your time, and aviate, navigate, and finally, communicate. Their questions will still exist after you complete the maneuver. The more important thing is that you are still alive and stable enough to answer them.

After the maneuvers, the flight should be relatively smooth sailing, but don't let your guard down just yet. A popular phrase in the aviation world is that "the checkride isn't over until the DPE is inside and shaking your hand, handing you a certificate." This is just as it sounds: don't act like the checkride is over just because you did amazingly at the maneuvers and the oral. You still have a landing, a taxi, and communications all the way until your engine is shut off. There are horror stories of pilots who did everything right—until they got on the ground and let down their guard, and before they knew it, they had accidentally switched radio frequencies or even worse, stopped following their checklists.

I say this out of caution, as you would not believe some of the silly mistakes that people make under pressure. According to confessions on Avweb dating back to 2014, confident pilots have failed for a variety of reasons: "The Cessna's door handle had been pushed to the down position, but the door was still open...the examiner instructed [the student] to taxi back to the ramp with a pink slip," reads one example of a checkride gone wrong. Another student flew an entire two hours in the wrong direction before realizing that they were lost about fifty miles away. "That was it, checkride busted. Mortified, I determined our location, the route home, and rescheduled the checkride." And to really drive the point home, a student getting ready for their tailwheel checkout flight was explicitly shown a broken propeller, told that it was the result of a landing with a tailwind, and then proceeded to taxi to the runway and set themselves up for a takeoff...with a tailwind.

So, don't be a horror story. Keep the good flying up until you get inside. Even more importantly, don't think you've failed unless the DPE says that you have failed—until you hear them say explicitly that you were unsatisfactory, remember that you still stand a chance to pass.

This advice was fantastic, especially for me. I thought I had failed my checkride early into the flight, but keeping this statement in mind, I knew I had to muster up my energy and continue onward with the rest of the tests. Despite the extra stress, I kept the plane in range and flew it professionally all the way down until I heard those magic words: "Let's get inside and get you your pilot's certificate." I'm telling you right now, I have never been more excited to pass a test in my life, and that remains true up to this day.

STEP 8: TELL PEOPLE YOU'RE A PILOT

"Whoa, hold on, so you're a pilot? Like, you fly planes? Real planes?"

As a pilot, that's a question you won't stop hearing. It fills you with pride each time—being able to bask in the glow of perceived excitement. And you should be proud; you moved mountains (or, at least, a significant sum of money) to be able to achieve this goal, not to mention the effort and time it takes to do so. At times, it may have felt like you couldn't overcome your challenges, but you stuck it out and worked your ass off—and before you know it, you're shaking your examiner's hand and posing with your newly issued Airman Certificate. Congratulations! As a certified private pilot, you can now literally look down on people.

From that point on, it's no longer a matter of what you just did, but a matter of why you continue to fly. You begin to answer for yourself: What is your favorite thing to do, and why is it flying? For some, it's being able to get places fast; for others, it's the pure opportunity that flying is able to give us. Flying is often referred to as the perfect romance hobby: it mixes our innate sense of adventure with the freedom of flight and the clout that comes with our certification to fly. This seems obvious to us as pilots, and even arguably to those who aren't pilots. So then, why is it that our numbers continue to drop? Why do general aviation pilots continue to decline? How can something so magnificent be so under pursued?

The act of flying itself is no small feat. When you begin driving a car, you can piece together what you should be doing because you've spent countless hours watching your parents drive—and as a result, you already have an intuition for when to stop, what to look out for, and where to speed up, slow down, and turn. In other words, you already have the base knowledge of a decent driver. But for a new student pilot, flying is fraught with different rules, regulations, and implications with which they don't have previous experience. As a result, there's a significant amount of knowledge that one must learn for oneself. Flying is not like driving: it's not always easy to know when to stop and go.

To drive this point home, I had the pleasure of working with Anna, a close friend and awesome pilot. Her story is a classic example of powering through the tough times and loving the freedom of flight.

"Since before I could walk, I always loved watching planes take off and land and would sit at the windowsill every night praying that I would sprout wings and be able to fly with the birds. I don't remember a time in my life where I wasn't obsessed and in love with flying."

No amount of waiting could hold Anna back, and she sums up her message to prospective pilots very well: "A passion is a passion for a reason, and I studied very hard, found opportunities and connections to get free ground school, and worked on my ground school knowledge while I waited to get money for the flying part. But it was all the more worth it knowing that I paid for the license myself, that I put all that work into it, and *earned* it rather than bought it. I think applying myself and writing essays for scholarships and all that waiting to get the funds for it made me realize that flying was something I loved and wanted to do, and it wasn't just a phase. In my journey, I have met so many people willing to help me with scholarships, ground school, free flying lessons, that it has made it so worth it and made me appreciate all the joys of being a pilot even more."

At the end of the day, that blueish-green card that comes in the mail after your final checkride is something to be proud of. It certifies not only the fact that you are capable of leaving the earth whenever you choose, but also that you have just scaled an absolute mountain of obstacles.

So why go through this chapter and tell you about all this? The answer is obvious! It's so you can maximize your chances of success at becoming a pilot. If you made it this far, you've already done it. You're one of the privileged few who now have their "license to learn." Now it can be your "fun fact" at parties or during breakout rooms over a Zoom call! Pro tip: you can also fly your friends around, which always makes for a fun birthday gift.

In all seriousness, you've accomplished an amazing feat. Less than one-tenth of a percent of humans can say the same. You did well. No, actually, you did fantastic. You went against the odds, stuck it out through thick and thin, and went and got your pilot's license. That, my friend, is what I call a success. And, now that I've been literally looking down at society for a few years, I figure I can share a thing or two about the experience—especially from the young, pilot-of-color perspective. The world of aviation is going through changes. As pilots, we should facilitate these changes to our industry and ensure that others get a chance at achieving their flying dreams. Becoming a pilot isn't just a fantasy anymore, it's a reality—and if you've managed to get your license, you know that. We, as pilots, need to adapt to a changing world and ensure that our love of flight isn't diminished, that it remains strong throughout our lifetimes and into the next. And the best way to do that, future aviators, is to address you, the next generation of pilots.

ACTION CHECKLIST:

- ☑ <u>Contact your flight school and schedule some block hours.</u>

- ☑ <u>Chair fly your flight lessons.</u>

- ☑ <u>Ask questions after each and every flight.</u>

- ☑ <u>Continue to attend your ground school and study.</u>

- ☑ <u>Pass the written exam.</u>

- ☑ <u>Solo!</u>

- ☑ <u>Fly well; don't crash.</u>

- ☑ <u>Finish your training.</u>

- ☑ <u>Practice your checkride.</u>

- ☑ <u>Mock oral.</u>

- ☑ Checkride maneuvers.

- ☑ More mock orals.

- ☑ Schedule your checkride.

- ☑ Pass!

- ☑ Fly well once again; don't crash once again.

- ☑ Go fly!

- ☑ Brag to everyone you meet!

CONCLUSION

When I began my journey as a pilot, I was completely blown away at how much I had to learn in such a short time and, quite honestly, how few resources there were for new pilots. Coming from a family where aviation didn't really exist (none of my relatives were pilots) meant having to learn how to navigate this path on my own, and it wasn't an easy path to trek. As I look back now, I recognize places where things could have gone better and where I could have saved myself some extra time, money, or hard work.

The primary reason I decided to write this book was a combination of wanting to share my story so others could avoid making my mistakes and highlighting all the good in the aviation community—as well as emphasizing that we still have a long way to go.

Like I mentioned before, getting your pilot's license is a massive task. The amount of new information that prospective pilots need to learn often causes many to hesitate. Add to that the lack of education, resources, and advocacy we need to inspire prospective pilots, and we have ourselves a stagnant industry.

To even have a chance at expanding the reach of our profession, the aviation community has to recognize the need to expand and encourage these new students to pursue their passions.

After reading this book, you're aware of the issues that challenge us today—systematic inequalities, discrimination, and high barriers to entry all impede progress in today's world above the clouds. This is not what we would expect from such a modernized society. The industry continues to represent a very narrow aspect of our population, which is concerning in a constantly evolving world. With astonishingly homogeneous statistics, it should be clear that as a community, we need to do more to get the next generation up above the clouds.

This book aims to give voice to some of those concerns, asking questions like: How can we continue to improve ourselves as an industry? How do we reconcile the problems of the world outside our aircraft with need for growth in our community? Lack of growth and diversity are certainly big beasts to tackle, and hopefully I was able to show you all some fantastic ways that some leading aviators are taking on that challenge.

There is no clear-cut answer to the above questions—no perfect solution. However, as pilots, it's important to consider that there are always ways to improve. We do that by advocating for aviation, educating future pilots, and ensuring that we pave a better path for success. It is that idea that I wanted to emphasize throughout this book.

After connecting and speaking with so many people within the aviation industry, I am very optimistic about the future of aviation. Finding so many people willing to support the continued advocacy of aviation was to be expected, but diving into their stories and plans for the future was awe-inspiring. Hearing how aviators of today are building up the next generation of pilots is in itself the essence of this book: how we approach and take on the challenges that currently face our community will define how the next generation shapes the industry itself.

Study after study demonstrates the need for diversity and the clear benefits that it provides us as a community, and as pilots and prospective students, we are all participants in the world of aviation. It will be the new ideas from these pilots that prove essential to the continuation and advancement of our passion.

In order for us to do that we need to make steps forward, not remain in our realm of relative comfort. Getting your license needs to be cheaper, and there need to be more programs that encourage young children to envision themselves in the cockpit. This book allowed me to highlight some of the ways the aviation community has been able to proceed with these changes.

As you're reading this, aviation advocacy programs promote flight as a viable opportunity for all students. They demonstrate to those even without close ties to the aeronautical world that they, too, can become a pilot. Programs like the local EAA chapters and Jesse Hayes's Red-Tailed Hawks show society that this is a real and lucrative place to be. Flight schools like Checkride Prep that generously remove the high barrier to entry encourage thousands to kick-start a dream they might have had in a previous stage of their lives. Thanks to these organizations we can inspire our new pilots: they provide the motivation, encouragement, and even the resources to accomplish this mission. Bottom line: they are truly getting the word out to the communities they serve, and we need more of them to truly ensure that our community grows and evolves.

Working together with advocacy programs are aviation education institutes, such as the Museum of Flight and Raisbeck Aviation High School, which help to prepare students to enter the industry and introduce them to industry mentors, pushing them toward higher education and career goals. We have organizations like these that enable pilots to be smarter, better prepared, and ready to take on the world of flight. These institutions accelerate the technology in the aircraft we fly so that we can be safer and so that we can leave a better footprint on our world as well. In many cases, like the Hillsboro Aero Academy, schools even offer a new way for pilots to enter the workforce, providing a clean, clear path to success.

We must recognize that it will not be the current generation that ensures the viability of aviation, but the next. With their new ideas and energy to continue improving upon the aviation community, they allow us to grow and learn as a whole. To make that happen, though, we must first make ourselves accessible. Through strong, concentrated efforts, we need to show young, diverse pilots that anyone can fly and that their childhood dreams are closer than they ever thought possible. We must allow them to envision not only a career in aviation but a seat for themselves in the cockpit of their very own aircraft. With our dedication toward their education, toward removing the inequities that stand in their way, and toward an overall awareness of the world above the clouds, we accomplish the goal of continuing our passion.

If you've ever thought about becoming a pilot, start your journey now. This book is your right of entry, an official invitation into one of the greatest communities in the world. Use the resources and guides you find here to reach out to a local aviators group, and get started today.

The next generation of pilots will shape the future of aviation for decades to come. Whether or not you contribute is up to you. If you do, I hope to fly with you in the sun above those cloudy ceilings soon. Blue skies!

ACKNOWLEDGMENTS

To all of my friends, my family, and supporters of this book that I have met along the way, thank you. To my parents, thank you for supporting me on this new and complex project. To the editing team at New Degree Press, thank you for supporting me throughout the process and constantly providing motivation to write. And to my friends, thank you for investing your time and money in me and this process. Your trust means a lot, and I would not have been able to do this without the support that you all have provided. This is the very first book that I have ever written, and there is absolutely no way that I could have gotten through this process without you all. It truly takes a village, and at the end of the day, I can say that each and every single one of you have helped me along a journey that I never thought I would start, let alone accomplish. You've all helped me actualize a fantastic goal, and I hope that one day I am able to repay the favor.

Special Thanks to My Early Supporters:

Don Hua, Thanh Loan Bui, Tija Marie, Braveen Mahendran, Sameer Romani, Lee Bui, Nathan Tran, Joseph Merlino, Brice

Van Buren, David Hadley, Jake O'Neill, Noelle Geddis, Wyatt Sitchin, Connie Gavin, Jack Gavin, Susan Enfield, Max Welliver, Alyssa Lam, Chris Medina, Janie Ng, Jackson Baker, Rachel Demaree, Noor Khan, Xhelan Sylve, Wayne Storer, Rishi Kutty, Erin Demaree, Therese Tipton, Michaela Nam, Grace Roberts, Michael Feehan, Marla Feehan, Peter Marsh, Joanne Yi, Theda Hiranaka, Brian Tran, D'Artagnan Heath, Nancy Caviezel, Micah Truman, Michael Gudor, Hazel H Bhang Barnett, Cooper Huck, Nikhil Joshi, Larry Nguyen, Scott McComb, Ramana Marshalla, Ryan Porter, Debi Beeson Tranholt, Marcie Wombold, Jay Novelo, Colter Korsmoe, Sam Korsmoe, Jesse Hayes IV, Nicholas Paris, Neil Jain, Sarah Sturtz, Charlie Clark, Olivia Gibson, Oliver Low, Lam Bui, Viet Q Tran, Calvin Huynh, Michae Fennell, Bob Dannenhold, Avery Cochrane, Matthew Hayes, Amrit Singh, David Tushin, Caroline Bromberg, Kate McPolin, E H Campisteguy, Darrin Morgan, Brandon Bowman, Nehema Kariuki, Caitlin Henning, Cooper LeComp, Alisha Tran, George Sidles IV, Naba Deyab, AnnaRose Beckett-Herbert, Najma Hashi, Selina Franovic, Brandon Aguilar, Evan Frishholz, Anna Horner, Chelsea Ho, Ray Bartlett, Minh Nguyen, Emma Kominars, Julio Rivera, Sarah Pagano, Sophia Goodson, Lorenzo Matheny, Kevin Tellez-Munoz, Zachary Bender-Kokx, Martin Vega Velasco, Rani Woerner, Alin Mustafat, Henry Feehan, Emily Tang, Riley Cain, Emily Pitcairn, Prisha Grover, Hong Ta, Joseph Nwizugbo, Charles Skinner, Eric Koester, Chase King, Phillip Johnson, Kliment Milanov, Reba Gilman, Addie Bowker, Benton Smith, Wren Bergin, and Alan Hernandez.

APPENDIX

———

INTRODUCTION

Data USA. "Aircraft Pilots & Flight Engineers | Data USA." Accessed August 17, 2020. https://datausa.io/profile/soc/aircraft-pilots-flight-engineers.

Bureau of Labor Statistics, US Department of Labor. "Labor Force Statistics From The Current Population Survey." Accessed August 17, 2020. https://www.bls.gov/cps/cpsaat11.htm

Pilot Institute (blog). "How Much Does It Cost To Become A Pilot?—Pilot Institute". November 19, 2019. Accessed August 17, 2020. https://pilotinstitute.com/pilot-license-cost/#:~:text=Most%20pilots%20require%2060%20to,and%20location%20among%20other%20factors

Murray, Geoff. "After Covid-19, Aviation Faces A Pilot Shortage". *Oliver Wyman,* 2021. https://www.oliverwyman.com/our-expertise/insights/2021/mar/after-covid-19-aviation-faces-a-pilot-shortage.html

CHAPTER 2

Pilot Institute. "Average Age Statistics of Pilots: Are We in a Pilot Shortage?" *Pilot Institute* (blog). February 14, 2020. Accessed May 5, 2021. https://pilotinstitute.com/pilot-age-statistics/

Biedenkapp, Patrick. "Why Is There A Lack Of Diversity In The Cockpit?" *Pilot Patrick* (blog). June 14, 2020. https://pilotpatrick. com/why-is-there-a-lack-of-diversity-in-the-cockpit/

US Department of Labor, Bureau of Labor Statistics. "Labor Force Statistics From The Current Population Survey." Accessed August 17, 2020. https://www.bls.gov/cps/cpsaat11.htm

."Expand Your Talent Base Through Diversity | NBAA—National Business Aviation Association." *Business Aviation Insider.* February 1, 2018. https://nbaa.org/professional-development/work-force-initiatives/expand-talent-base-diversity/

Negroni, Christine. "How Much Of The World's Population Has Flown In An Airplane?" *Air & Space Magazine.* January 6, 2016. https://www.airspacemag.com/daily-planet/how-much-worlds-population-has-flown-airplane-180957719/

Masters, Charlie. "Breaking The Barriers, The Final 4 Obstacles To Your Flight Training—Student Pilot News." *Sporty's Student Pilot News* (blog). March 28, 2014. https://studentpilotnews. com/2014/03/28/breaking-barriers-final-4-obstacles-flight-training/

Metsker, Meredith. "Pilot Shortage: Three Reasons Why The U.S. Is Running Out Of Pilots." *Emsi* (blog). May 24, 2018. https://economicmodeling.com/2018/05/24/pilot-shortage-three-reasons-why-us-running-out-of-pilots/

Statista. "Number Of Drivers Licensed In The US 2019 | Statista."
2020. *Statista*. Accessed June 17, 2021. https://www.statista.com/
statistics/191653/number-of-licensed-drivers-in-the-us-since-
1988/#:~:text=Almost%20230%20million%20people%20held,-
wheel%20is%2016%20years%20old

Ostrower, Jon. "The U.S. Will Face A Staggering Shortage Of Pilots."
CNN. July 27, 2017. https://money.cnn.com/2017/07/27/news/com-
panies/pilot-shortage-figures/index.html

CAE. "Pilot Outlook Demand—Summary | CAE." Accessed June
19, 2021. https://www.cae.com/cae-pilot-demand-outlook-2020/

Smith, Morgan. "Black Female Pilot Starts Initiative To Enroll 100
Black Women In Flight School." *People Magazine*. April 8, 2021.
https://people.com/human-interest/black-female-pilot-56-starts-
initiative-to-enroll-100-black-women-in-flight-school/

Aircraft Owners and Pilots Association. "The Flight Training
Experience." AOPA, 2010. https://download.aopa.org/epilot/2011/
AOPA_Research-The_Flight_Training_Experience.pdf

United Airlines. "United Sets New Diversity Goal: 50% Of Students At New Pilot Training Academy To Be Women And People Of Color." United Airlines press release, April 6, 2021. United
Airlines United Hub website. https://hub.united.com/2021-04-
06-united-sets-new-diversity-goal-50-of-students-at-new-pilot-
training-academy-to-be-women-and-people-of-color-2651374725.
html, accessed June 15, 2021.

Wahl, Christoph. "OPINION: Diversity In Airline Leadership
Brings Success." *Flight Global*. January 29, 2016. https://www.

flightglobal.com/opinion/opinion-diversity-in-airline-leader-ship-brings-success/119488.article

US Department of Transportation, Federal Aviation Administration. "Why STEM?" Accessed June 15, 2021. https://www.faa.gov/education/why_stem/

CHAPTER 4

US Department of Transportation, Federal Aviation Administration. "Air Traffic By The Numbers." Accessed May 9, 2021. https://www.faa.gov/air_traffic/by_the_numbers/

Experimental Aircraft Association. "Experimental Aircraft Information." Accessed May 15, 2021. https://www.eaa.org/eaa/about-eaa/eaa-media-room/experimental-aircraft-information

Thurber, Matt. "The Aircraft Certification Process." *Aviation International News*. December 18, 2006. https://www.ainonline.com/aviation-news/aviation-international-news/2006-12-18/air-craft-certification-process

CHAPTER 5

Museum of Flight. "Our Mission." Accessed June 28, 2021. https://www.museumofflight.org/About-Us/mission

CHAPTER 6

Red Tailed Hawks Flying Club. "Donate." Accessed June 28, 2021. https://redtailedhawksflyingclub.org/donate/

CHAPTER 7

Aircraft Owners and Pilots Association. "The Flight Training Experience." AOPA, 2010. https://download.aopa.org/epilot/2011/ AOPA_Research-The_Flight_Training_Experience.pdf

CHAPTER 8

Pimentel, Dan. "Is A Sport Certificate Right For You?" *Flying Magazine*. March 24, 2020. https://www.flyingmag.com/story/training/ learn-to-fly-sport-pilot-certificate/

CHAPTER 9

Berge, Paul. "Checkride Disasters." *AvWeb*. May 5, 2014. https:// www.avweb.com/features/checkride-disasters/

Blair, Jason. "Initial Pilot Certification Passing Rates Trending Down." *Avweb*. May 22, 2018. https://www.avweb.com/flight-safety/technique/initial-pilot-certification-passing-rates-trending-down/

US Department of the Interior, National Aeronautics and Space Administration. "Human Factors Of Flight-Deck Checklists: The Normal Checklist" by Degani, Asaf, and Earl L. Wiener. Mountain View, California, 1990. https://ti.arc.nasa.gov/m/profile/adegani/ Flight-Deck_Checklists.pdf

US Department of Transportation, Federal Aviation Administration. "Airmen Certification Standards FAQs." Accessed May 27, 2021. https://www.faa.gov/training_testing/testing/acs/media/ acs_faq.pdf

Bell, Catherine. "Using Checklists To Prevent Failure". *Harvard Business Review,* January 21, 2010. In *HBR IdeaCast.* Produced by Catherine Bell. Podcast, 15:50. https://hbr.org/2010/01/using-checklists-to-prevent-fa.html

Boldmethod (blog). "What To Expect On Your Private Pilot Check-ride: The Oral Exam." August 25, 2020. Accessed May 22, 2021. https://www.boldmethod.com/blog/article/2020/08/what-to-expect-on-your-private-pilot-checkride-oral-exam/

CHAPTER 10

Aircraft Owners and Pilots Association. "AOPA Flight Training Scholarship Applications Now Open." Aircraft Owners and Pilots Association press release, December 15, 2020. Aviation Pros website. https://www.aviationpros.com/education-training/press-release/21202647/aircraft-owners-and-pilots-association-aopa-aopa-flight-training-scholarship-applications-now-open, accessed May 27, 2021.

Aircraft Owners and Pilots Association. "The Flight Training Experience." AOPA, 2010. https://download.aopa.org/epilot/2011/AOPA_Research-The_Flight_Training_Experience.pdf

Take on College. "Resources." Accessed June 29, 2021. https://www.takeoncollege.org/resources

Post University (blog). "Wondering Why Scholarships Are Important?" February 19, 2021. Accessed June 3, 2021. https://post.edu/blog/wondering-why-scholarships-are-important/#:~:text=Here's%20why%20scholarships%20are%20important,to%20focus%20on%20their%20studies